W9-CZJ-586

Mastering Medical Sales

The Essential Attitudes, Habits, and Skills of High-earning Medical Sales Professionals

Mace Horoff
Healthcare Business Books

Library of Congress Control Number: 2009911025

Includes index
ISBN-13: 9780-6153-3035-8
ISBN-10: 0-6153-3035-5

For additional copies contact:
Sales Pilot Medical Sales Training
Phone: (561) 333-8080
http://www.MedicalSalesTraining.com
http://www.MasteringMedicalSales.com

Published by:
Healthcare Business Books
P.O. Box 212931
Royal Palm Beach, Florida 33421-2931
Printed in the United States of America

Edited by Brenda Robinson
Cover design by Ken Harman
Inside design and formatting by Dawn Von Strolley Grove

*To the medical sales professionals in the world
who honor this noble profession
by selling with integrity.*

The more you sweat at practice, the less you bleed in battle.

—Author Unknown

Contents

Warning—Disclaimer

This book is designed to provide information in regard to the subject matter covered. It is sold with the understanding that the publisher and authors and advisors are not rendering legal, accounting or other professional services. If legal or other expert assistance is required, the services of a competent professional should be sought.

The authors and publishers make no representations or warranties with respect to the accuracy or completeness of the contents of this book and specifically disclaim any implied warranties or merchantability or fitness for a particular purpose. No warranty may be created or extended by sales representatives or written sales materials. The advice and strategies contained herein may not be suitable for your situation. Neither the publisher nor author shall be liable for any loss of profit, commercial damages, or legal actions, including but not limited to special, incidental, consequential, or other damages caused, or alleged to have been caused, directly or indirectly, by the information contained in this book.

It is not the purpose of this book to provide information or advice on the laws and regulations that govern healthcare at the federal, state, local, or any level. References to any laws, rules, or regulations should not be construed as the actual laws, rules, or regulations. It is the responsibility of the reader to know and comply with any and all rules that govern the sales of medical devices, equipment, pharmaceuticals, biotechnology products and any other products sold for use in treating patients or delivering patient care if he or she is engaged in selling such products to healthcare institutions, providers, and suppliers.

This book is not intended to provide healthcare compliance training. If assistance is required with respect to healthcare compliance issues, expert assistance should be sought.

While the stories used in this book are based on real events, the names of people, companies, and institutions used are not the real names. Any resemblance or similarities to real people, corporate entities, businesses or institutions is not intended and is purely coincidental.

Every effort has been made to make this book as complete and as accurate as possible. However, there *may be mistakes*, both typographical and in content. Therefore, this text should be used only as a general guide and not as the ultimate source of medical sales information.

Introduction

I never wanted to be a salesman. In my mind, salesmen were pushy people who coerced others into buying what they were selling, whether it was needed or not. It seemed like sales became the default vocation for those who did not have the skills to do anything else. Selling was never high on anyone's career list. How many times have you heard a child say, "I want to be a salesman when I grow up?" I never did.

So how did I become a medical sales professional? It happened by circumstance.

I was a graduate student in anatomy and thoroughly enjoyed my first year studying gross anatomy, embryology, and histology. One of my responsibilities was to teach gross anatomy to medical and dental students and believed I had found my calling. However, being a professor of anatomy involved doing research, and I quickly discovered during year two that I did not like the isolation of the research laboratory–I need to be around people. It was time to find another career.

My only worthwhile paid employment up until this point was working in a hospital pathology department assisting with autopsies and processing surgical specimens. I found the work interesting, but again, not much interaction with people . . . at least *living* people. Someone suggested that I become a nuclear medicine technologist, a healthcare professional who uses specialized scanning instruments and radioisotopes that are injected, swallowed, or inhaled to diagnose and treat disease. It sounded interesting, the field was expanding, plus my knowledge of anatomy would be useful. I breezed through the academic and didactic part of the training and accepted a position as a staff technologist at a hospital in Miami. It was fun for about a year, but after a few thousand liver, bone and brain scans, it got old. I was bored, and although I earned a reasonable income, I wanted to earn more.

While perusing the help wanted section of the Sunday paper, I noticed an ad for a nuclear medicine technologist with an *entrepreneurial spirit* to operate a mobile nuclear cardiac scanning service in Atlanta. I didn't want to leave Florida, but the salary was almost double what I was earning at the hospital, and I craved a new challenge. Within a ten day period, I mailed a resume, flew up for an interview, and got the job.

The company was almost ready to begin operations. They had just received the necessary operational licenses and permits prior to my arrival. The new scanner had been delivered, and I travelled to New York for two days to receive training on how to operate it. I returned to Atlanta, all fired up and ready to get down to business. There was only one thing missing—we had no physicians lined-up to refer patients.

The CEO of the company told me that he had interviewed several experienced medical sales representatives to sell our service to cardiologists and oncologists. When he shared with me that these salespeople all wanted a guaranteed salary of $80,000 to $100,000 per year, I was stunned. I asserted, "Where do they come off thinking that they are worth that kind of money?" The CEO shrugged and responded,

"That's what experienced medical sales reps earn, and some earn much more than that."

I now understood how many of the sales reps that I met while working in the hospital were able to afford the good life. They wore nice suits and jewelry, often talked about houses in prime locations, boats, company cars, dining at expensive restaurants and trips to exotic places that I could not afford to visit. I gathered that they did pretty well financially, but I had no idea that they did *that* well!

Feeling a surge of confidence, I said to the CEO, "I've got an idea. I have a lot of experience working with doctors. I speak their language— I'm familiar with anatomy and pathology. You're already paying me, and without doctors referring patients for me to scan, I have nothing else to do. What do you think about letting me call on some local doctors to see if I can bring in some business? I think I can do the selling and save the company from having to guarantee some salesman a large salary?"

The CEO liked my idea, but asked me to meet with the company's medical director to find out if the doctor thought I was up to the task, and to make sure he was comfortable with me selling to his colleagues. The meeting went well, and the medical director handed me a list of cardiologists and oncologists who had expressed an interest in the company's services. Through a combination of circumstance and sudden ambition, *I was in medical sales.*

After calling to schedule appointments, and buying a new suit at J.C. Penney (the only credit card I had), I went on my first sales calls. My idea of selling was to shake each doctor's hand, and then tell him everything I could think of regarding our service, hoping that he would say "yes." A few of the physicians, who were good friends with our medical director, offered to schedule some patients to try us out.

However, the other doctors I met with threw so many reasons at me not to use our service (my first experience dealing with sales objections) that I just wanted to run out of their office and never go back. I was the proverbial *fish out of water*, and had never felt so rejected. Not only did I doubt my ability to sell, but I started to doubt the viability of the service I was offering. But I had appealed to the CEO and the medical director to let me be their sales rep and I was not eager to admit failure. It also occurred to me that without doctors sending us patients, the company could go out of business and I would be out of a job. Returning to a position as a staff technologist in a hospital somewhere did not appeal to me.

One Friday night, in an attempt to escape my frustration, I visited a bookstore. As I walked past the business books, a title caught my eye—it was, "How to Master the Art of Selling," by Tom Hopkins[1]. As I curiously paged through the book, I learned for the first time that there was a process and a psychology to selling. With renewed hope, I bought the book, went home and literally stayed up all night reading it from cover-to-cover. The new excitement I felt about selling overwhelmed me. I couldn't wait to make my next sales call!

I was closing more sales, but not as many as I had hoped. Enrolling in an eight-week sales training program taught me more sales skills, but many were not appropriate for selling to physicians. It became a trial-and-error process to discover which selling approaches worked and which ones didn't, but in time I was getting more and more physicians to use our mobile cardiac scanning service. I soon realized that I enjoyed selling so much that I wanted to do it full-time, so I turned in my resignation. I agreed to remain with the company for a few more months until they could hire a technologist to replace me, then I began

---

[1] Hopkins, Tom. *How to Master the Art of Selling.* Scottsdale Arizona: Champion Press, 1980, 1982

my search for a full-time medical sales position. Six months later I landed a job selling surgical implants. Finally, I had found the right career!

I was immersed in medical sales for the next twenty-plus years and quickly learned that many of the sales techniques that work quite well in other industries can get you thrown out of a doctor's office or hospital with instructions not to come back. Healthcare providers are experts in their respective fields. They think differently and buy differently, and the sales person who doesn't understand these differences and sell accordingly is doomed to limited success. Those sales people who manage to stay in the job will probably learn the ins and outs of medical sales on their own, but the learning curve can be frustrating and painful.

Mastering Medical Sales is not based on theory or information from other sales books—it is derived from decades of interacting with some of the highest paid medical sales professionals in the country plus my own experience selling and training others to sell to hospitals, clinics, physicians from multiple medical and surgical specialties, dentists, therapists, laboratories, and other healthcare providers and support personnel. As you read through the chapters, some of the approaches and techniques discussed will seem fairly simple, and they are—once you have practiced and perfected your ability to use them. Learning to sell in the medical arena is like learning to land an airplane–it seems fairly easy when you read about it, but I can tell you from experience, the first few times you actually try to put an airplane on a runway, it can be downright frightening . . . and you will make some bad landings. If you just keep doing the right things, sooner or later you will get the results you want, and it will eventually become second nature. This book is designed to shorten the learning curve for new medical sales representatives and to help experienced sales reps reach the next level of success.

I am grateful to have worked in such a dynamic industry with so many dedicated healthcare providers and highly motivated sales professionals. Now, as a speaker, trainer, author, and consultant, I get to help others succeed in medical sales so that the products and services they represent can make a difference for their healthcare customers and their customer's patients.

Mace Horoff

Nothing is more important than the patient.
Whatever you do in your medical sales career,
the patient must always be your first
and most important consideration.

1

Why Medical Sales As A Career?

People enter into a medical sales career for many reasons. You should begin by asking yourself why you are currently engaged in or considering medical sales.

The most common reason for people to enter medical sales is for a challenging job that offers good financial compensation. The field also carries the prestige of working in a professional medical environment, avoiding the often negative stereotype of sales in other industries.

But, medical sales is still sales, and not everyone is equipped to succeed in this vocation. Any type of selling requires the ability to handle rejection on a daily basis and still continue moving forward. Those who persevere, despite ever-present obstacles, will be rewarded over time with a loyal clientele and generous commissions.

People who choose medical sales as a career should do so only after a careful assessment of their personalities, skill sets and interests. Let's examine each one individually.

Personality traits

Salespeople usually tend to be confident, friendly and outgoing. Their need for confidence is obvious. You must believe that you will ultimately succeed and that your product or service is the best choice for your prospective customers. The medical professionals to whom you sell can detect a lack of confidence from a mile away. They want to do business with someone who bolsters their confidence in the choices that they make for treating their patients. Confidence is either something you have or need to develop. Without it, you will be dead in the water.

Many go into sales because they enjoy working with people. Surprisingly, there are some salespeople who don't seem especially sociable. These paradoxes are easily resolved, because most people do not like them and they are not successful in sales. It is amazing how many people I have met who work in medical sales that are not personable, and yet they can't understand why they aren't doing well. The bottom line is that people will do business with people they like and avoid doing business with people they don't.

Many salespeople think that they can fake friendliness, but they can't! Most people can spot a phony a mile away. The salespeople who fake friendliness can only carry on the charade during the sale. Once the sale is made or in-between calls, their true personalities come out. Merely bringing your customers gifts (accepting gifts and favors from salespeople is now prohibited in most areas of health care) is not what it means to be friendly. If you don't have a genuine interest in others or care about them as people, you will not be perceived as friendly.

A key trait of successful medical sales professionals is that they truly like to help people. When you do your job well, many people will benefit, but it begins by caring about your health care provider customers and their patients. Never forget, the ultimate beneficiary of anyone who works in the healthcare industry is the patient. Countless patients' lives are better because of the caring medical sales people who were there to help the medical professionals to do the best job possible.

Skill sets

Successful medical salespeople possess certain skills and abilities that allow them to excel. If you're in sales, those who know you may have once said: "You're great with people—you should go into sales." What they observed in you are skills and abilities that allow you to easily establish a rapport with people and communicate effectively.

The most recognizable skill of good salespeople is the ability to speak well. Successful salespeople are articulate and always seem to be able to find the right words for any occasion. They are not only good at speaking, they truly enjoy it. In fact, the new salesperson is usually champing at the bit to get out and make the first sales presentation, because he or she loves to speak.

Don't confuse the habit of being a "good talker" with the necessary skill of being a professional presenter. Strong presentation skills are one of the primary traits separating the true sales professional from the amateur. You must be a good communicator and know how to structure your presentation in a way that your prospects and customers will understand the benefits of your offering.

Active listening

Another important hallmark of a good presenter is the ability to be an active listener. You must encourage your prospects and customers to talk about the products or services they need to perform their jobs and care for their patients. But, if you're not listening, you won't hear what they are saying, so good listening skills are essential.

One of the keys to understanding sales presentation skills is knowing that "selling is not telling." After listening to and coaching myriad sales presentations over the years, I can say with confidence that up to 90 percent of all salespeople don't fully understand this concept. A sales presentation is an interactive exchange of information. If you rate your selling skills by your ability to memorize and regurgitate your company's promotional material, you will only be deceiving yourself.

Organization

An important trait in any type of sales, but especially in medical sales, is the ability to be an enterprising self-starter. Managing your territory is like running a small business. While you will probably be held responsible to a supervisor, what you do on a day-to-day basis is usually up to you. You must be highly organized and cultivate good time management skills. You should be the kind of person who decides what they are going to do on a given day long before they wake up.

Good self-starters have clearly defined goals and a detailed action plan to accomplish those goals. Almost everything in the medical environment is time sensitive, so enterprising salespeople set reasonable deadlines to achieve their goals.

Decisiveness

Decision-making is a crucial skill for medical sales. The ability to decide on a course of action is critical when you consider the immediacy and high stakes inherent in this field. Remember too, that in this environment you are often operating independently. I have learned that the only thing worse than making the wrong decision is making no decision. Leaving important events to chance only demonstrates a lack of control over your environment. Customers will respect you more for making an occasional bad choice then they will for just allowing things to happen on their own. Of course, once you develop good decision-making skills, you will be more confident about making decisions.

Selling requires a willingness to take risks. The practice of medicine is often a balancing act of risks and rewards. As a provider of products and services to the medical community, both you and your company share some of that risk. Generally, your company covers the liability risk for the services or products that it offers, but to succeed in medical sales, you will need to take some risks of a more personal nature. Sometimes, it will be necessary for you to think or act "out-of-the-box" to move a sale forward or even to attract the interest of a prospective customer. Each time, you will risk rejection and damage to your ego, but the potential for large rewards usually offsets the risk in the medical sales field. The bottom line, though, is that you mustn't be averse to handling some risk on a daily basis.

Personal interest

Many people choose medical sales as a career because it is so interesting to them. The marvels of medicine and working with the human body can provide an endless source of mental stimulation. Any interest in science or engineering is helpful, because selling medical products often involves aspects of these disciplines.

Specialized expertise

Expertise in the field is not an option, but an absolute requirement for the products or services that you will be offering to your customers and it is easier to develop this knowledge when you have a natural interest in something. Interest leads to passion, and when you express passion for your product, your customers will sense that, increasing the chances for a sale. This factor alone can give you a huge advantage over any competitors who sell only with a commission in mind.

The medical device, pharmaceutical and biotechnology industries offer a range of opportunities that will satisfy a variety of interests. It is vitally important to find an area that interests you to maximize your success. Don't settle for less, because you will find it.

Monetary compensation

I have left money for last, but for most people, compensation is their main reason for going into medical sales. There is no question that medical sales can offer a great long-term income potential. When you possess the requisite skill sets, there are few places that you can earn the level of income that you can in medical sales. Most people will tolerate the hard work and dedication required if they are well-paid, and in medical sales, you will be.

Medical sales however, can be either a very high-paying job or a very low-paying one, depending on the performance of the salesperson. Generally, if you are meeting the sales quota expectations of your company, you'll be earning the income you anticipated when you accepted the position. If you exceed the quota, you'll earn more. But those salespeople who fail to meet the challenge or do not maintain the needed discipline will be disappointed, and so will their employers.

Earning potential

The one question that everyone wants to know about medical sales is, "How much can you earn?" Because of the volatile nature of any economy, it makes sense to discuss the various compensation plans than it does to present actual figures.

Salary plus bonus: This is one of the most common compensation plans, in which salespeople receive a guaranteed salary with the opportunity to earn more, based on performance. The additional money is usually paid in the form of a bonus that can be paid when the salesperson reaches or exceeds their quota. When bonuses are paid for exceeding quota, the amount is often based on the percentage by which the quota was exceeded. The salary plus bonus plan works well because it motivates the salesperson to achieve the company's goal, but also to obtain bonuses by exceeding their quota, providing added income for both parties.

Salary plus commission: Some medical companies pay a salary plus commission. This means that the salesperson is paid a base salary plus a percentage of any of the gross sales in his or her territory. The base salary allows the salesperson to meet his or her expenses and earn additional income through superior sales efforts.

Straight commission: Many of the higher incomes in medical sales are earned through straight commissions. Those who work on straight commission are paid a percentage of the gross sales only when a sale is consummated. Industry jargon for this method is that, "You eat what you kill!" Obviously, there is an upside to this and a downside.

Let's look at the downside first. Some people starting out may accept a territory that has little or no business. If you are working on straight commission, you will be paid only on what you sell, and unless you have a draw or guarantee, your compensation could be pretty stark.

A draw is a defined amount of income paid for a period of time, e.g., a week or month, which will be repaid as commissions are earned that exceed the draw. The thing to remember is that a draw needs to be paid back. A guarantee is a defined amount of guaranteed income that does not need to be repaid. Should the commissions total less than the guarantee, the salesperson will still be paid the guaranteed amount. This practice, however, is not likely to be prolonged.

This is often how many salespeople with little or no experience begin their careers, because by agreeing to work on straight commission, they limit the financial risk to their companies. Keep in mind that to start, you may be eating a lot of macaroni and cheese until your sales start to increase.

The upside to working on straight commission is that when your sales are high, your commissions are high. It is usually not necessary for you to hit a certain level of sales volume to earn additional income, although some compensation plans increase the commission percentage after reaching a defined sales volume. Again, most high-earning medical sales professionals work on straight commission.

Part of the compensation plan in medical sales can include benefits such as health insurance, disability insurance, retirement programs and a company car. The value of these benefits can quickly add up. Benefit packages are provided to salespeople who are employees of the company, as opposed to independent contractors. There are situations where independent contractors may have the opportunity to buy benefits at reduced rates through the companies they represent, but salespeople who earn straight commission usually provide their own benefits and car.

While it is money that draws people to medical sales and keeps them there, is not a means to an end. Medical sales can be hard work, both physically and mentally, and if you are not enjoying the career, you risk burning out, and the ability to maintain incremental sales increases diminishes. This usually means earning less money, and if it is money that keeps you in the job, you've got trouble. So, it's important to land a job that not only pays well, but that you will look forward to doing every day.

If you work on straight commission, it is important to remember that there will be "rainy days." In good times, when the commission dollars are flowing in and you are working really hard, it's easy to reward yourself by spending equally hard. I'm not saying that you should not reward yourself with a nice vacation, a new car, a boat, a new watch, or whatever your heart desires. Just remember to make allowances for times where your commissions may decrease due to circumstances that are out of your control. Make sure you build up a cash reserve to get you through those rainy days, and you will sleep better at night. The best advice I could give is to always try and live below your means. You will always work and perform better when financial pressures do not burden you.

Summary

It is the sum total of personality, skills, interests and a desire for money that drives people into medical sales. Regardless of the reasons you are considering or have chosen this profession, you must continuously assess your skills and attitude to be sure you are up to the challenge. The skills that allow people to succeed in medical sales can be learned and can always be improved. Whenever you invest time, money or a combination of both to improve your job performance, it will pay huge dividends.

Medical sales demands a huge personal commitment from the day you begin your career until the day you retire, but you can always expect to reap great rewards if you work hard and commit to being the best you can be.

2

Selling in Healthcare is Different

I frequently get calls from people who are trying to break into medical sales. Some ask whether their sales experience in a particular industry will transfer to the medical arena. Others assume that "sales is sales" and just want to know how to get hired.

While there are many similarities between selling in healthcare and selling in other industries, make no mistake — there are many significant differences, too. I have worked with people who sold automobile parts, beauty equipment, food products and even cemetery plots. Some of these salespeople quickly adapted to medical sales, while others were less successful.

During training, I always place the participants in a realistic simulated medical sales environment. One trainee, Bob, was hired by a dental supply company. Bob sold cars for 15 years, and in the sales simulations, I realized that his success in automobile sales stemmed from his willingness to pounce on the customer, like a lion on a fresh piece of meat. He would start "closing" within 30 seconds of meeting the prospect and ask for the business continuously throughout the presentation. That worked for selling cars, but this approach will not work very well with healthcare professionals. Yes, at some point you need to ask for the business (not always –we'll cover that in a later chapter)—but not before you have confirmed or helped the customer establish the need for what you are selling.

The flip side of the coin is people, often with some type of clinical medical experience, with zero sales experience. During their medical careers, they may have worked with medical sales professionals who make the job look easy. In their minds, selling medical equipment is nothing more than telling the prospective customer everything you know about your product, but it's not that simple. Clinical and product knowledge alone are not enough to succeed in medical sales.

One thing I have observed about successful medical sales professionals is that more of them hail from sales backgrounds than from clinical backgrounds. That's because it is easier to teach someone clinical and product knowledge than it is to teach them how to sell. Medical companies have recognized this for years, and it is one of the key reasons that, next to someone with a history of successful medical sales, companies will often hire candidates with business-to-business sales experience.

So, you can sell. Great! What makes medical sales so different from selling cars, postal meters or insurance? The customer. A medical buyer, regardless of position, is making decisions that directly affect clinical outcomes and thus, people's lives. Don't misunderstand; a purchasing agent will be shopping from a perspective very different from a physician's. But there is more at stake than buying something that someone will use, as opposed to something that will be used on someone. Ultimately, healthcare providers are responsible for patients' welfare, and that includes making informed, intelligent decisions about the products and services they buy.

If the medical sales professional understands how and why selling in medicine is different, it becomes clear why many of the approaches commonly used in non-medical selling are inappropriate.

Let's go back to our salesman trainee, Bob. Despite my best efforts, Bob's selling behavior did not change once he got out into the field. He had difficulty because sales managers in the car business are always telling their employees to "push a little harder." As I followed up via conference calls, he mentioned that many of his customers told him that he was too pushy, and that's not the way they buy. Bob has moved on to find a sales career better matched to his selling style.

Medicine is a scientific discipline that deals with facts. Healthcare providers need to analyze the available data about products and services and reach a decision based on careful consideration of all the variables. This requires working with a salesperson who understands their thought process and that time is necessary to make these decisions. In medical sales, we don't ask, "Doctor, what do I need to do to sell you this pacemaker today?"

Coming to medical sales from a clinical background, many professionals mistakenly believe that medical selling is just a matter of memorizing product knowledge and telling a client about how that product works. Often, this interpretation results from them witnessing only part of the selling process—an evaluation or demonstration. All of the data gathering, observation and analysis, a critical step before delivering the information, is unseen. The inexperienced see a medical sales representative as someone who just talks about the product—and that looks easy. Of course, real professionals always make it look easy.

Unfortunately, most of the clinical people I know who moved to medical sales moved back to a clinical position within a year or two. Dan, a clinical materials coordinator in an operating room for 14 years, went to work selling for an instrument company. Nine months later, he was back in the O.R. He said, "Mace, I have a new respect for what you guys do. I can't do it." I tried talking to Dan about taking the steps to learn the business, but for him, it was over. He was a fish out of water and the experience of rejection was too painful.

Here's the good news. If you do come from a clinical background or from selling outside of medicine—you can learn effective approaches that will pave your way to success in medical sales. To do that, you may need to step out of your comfort zone. It's not going to be easy, and you may get your "nose bloodied," but once you get past the learning curve, you will have a stable, financially rewarding career. Let's look more closely at what makes selling in medicine different.

Doctors, Hospitals and the Business of Medicine

When it comes to patient care, the healthcare provider and healthcare institution are the decision-makers (along with the patient, of course—but not from a buying perspective). By healthcare provider, I refer to any medical professional, such as a doctor, nurse, therapist, etc. An institution is a hospital, clinic, or other facility that provides treatment and associated services for patients. Whether you sell to the doctor directly, a hospital, clinic, or a buying consortium, it is often the healthcare provider or a group of healthcare providers and associated personnel who decide whether or not your product or service is purchased.

The single most important buying criterion should always be what is best for the patient. Unfortunately, this is not always the case, as there are many factors that enter into the equation. But one of the key selling points for any product or service you offer must be that it offers more to the providers of care and the patient than what is currently in use.

Traditionally, the physician had the final say regarding what products and services were used to treat his or her patient, so if you developed strong relationships with the doctors and knew how to sell to them, you would be successful in medical sales. This is no longer the case.

Product and service selection is often decided or approved by a committee, comprised of not only healthcare professionals, but other employees of hospitals and clinics whose interests may be very different from those that provide patient care directly. The ability to influence a doctor's decision is often insufficient; you need to be able to sell to the entire decision-making group.

Medical sales might seem as simple as going into a medical facility, demonstrating your solution as superior to the status quo, and voila—a slam dunk, but it's not that simple; other factors enter into play. For example, a doctor choosing a specific product to treat a patient may need to balance what is best for the patient against what is best for the hospital and healthcare system overall.

The hospital is a community, and all of the people who work there, including physicians, are expected to be good citizens. This means supporting the ultimate goals of the hospital, which includes providing care in a cost-effective way. Much of what goes on in the hospital-physician relationship is *quid pro quo*. There are things that each party must provide to the other for their mutual success. The sales representative must understand these relationships and implement sales strategies that benefit both parties, when necessary.

Let's consider a heart surgeon, Dr. Smith, who just joined the staff at XYZ Hospital. Dr. Smith has extensive training on a machine that is used to perform minimally invasive heart procedures and wants the hospital to invest in one of these machines, at a cost of $1.5 million. The hospital will conduct a feasibility study, either formally or informally, to determine if this is a good investment and good liability decision for the hospital.

Here are some of the questions that the hospital will consider before agreeing to purchase the machine:

- Are the procedures that Dr. Smith will perform considered safe and effective?
- Are the outcomes as good as or better than those of the procedures being performed at the hospital without the new machine?
- Will the procedure using the new machine provide a marketing approach that will bring more patients and generate more revenue and profits for the hospital?
- Does the machine increase the liability exposure for the hospital?
- Will Dr. Smith admit patients preferentially to XYZ Hospital, or will he be supporting another hospital, as well?
- Will Dr. Smith support the hospital's buying decisions in terms of the other products that he uses to treat his patients?

Let's consider that last point. Say for example, that the hospital stocks an artificial heart valve manufactured by the ABC Heart Valve Company. Dr. Smith has trained with a heart valve made by the DEF Heart Valve Company, which he considers to be a better valve for his patients. The cost of the DEF heart valve is 20 percent higher than the ABC heart valve, which can translate into the hospital spending another $100,000 per year on a procedure with a fixed reimbursement. In other words, they lose $100K in profits. Will Dr. Smith compromise and use the lower cost valve to save the hospital money? He might, if it is a factor that determines whether or not he will get his new machine.

This example shows that even when the doctor gets to choose products for his patients, and has or should have his patient's best interest at heart, there may be other factors influencing the decision. These may be factors you are not going to know about, at least initially, so a good understanding of the politics of medicine must be considered in your sales approach. Just keep in mind that understanding each buyer's thought process is critically important.

The Business of Medicine

If you are going to sell medical products and services, you must understand the business of medicine, including the various profit centers for the doctor and the hospital or clinic, and how everyone gets paid, including the company that you represent.

Reimbursement is a huge issue for hospitals and opportunities exist for companies that can reduce the overall cost of medical care with products or services. A salesperson must be able to demonstrate this ability on several levels, because much more comes into play than the purchase price of the product or service itself. For example:

- Will your product or service reduce the overall cost of treatment in terms of man-hours, days in the hospital, recovery time, fewer future procedures and hospital/doctor visits?
- Will the use of your product be reimbursed by private insurance or Medicare/Medicaid?
- Will it provide a doctor with more time to treat more patients?
- Can your product reduce the doctor's and hospital's liability exposure?

Government Regulation and Compliance

Another thing that makes selling in medicine different is that the field is heavily regulated. The Food and Drug Administration (FDA) determines what products are approved for medical use and in what ways, imposing strict rules as to how products can be sold. The penalty for violating these rules can be severe, both for the seller and the buyer.

When you sell in the medical environment, not only what you say, but to whom and how you say it, are critical regulatory issues. A lack of attention to these details on the part of a copier salesperson has few implications, but it could land a medical sales professional in federal court. Maintaining a constant awareness of current regulations in your sales efforts is a necessary way of life.

In recent years, the Department of Justice has charged manufacturers and healthcare entities with violating federal healthcare laws and levied fines totaling hundreds of millions of dollars. Doctors and hospitals, medical product distributors, and even salespeople have endured long investigations and paid fines. Some regulations carry criminal penalties, including incarceration. A working knowledge of compliance issues in today's healthcare environment is more than just handy—it's essential.

Buyers' Loyalty

As in any other industry, buyer loyalty exists in healthcare and can be either good or bad news, depending on whether or not the customer is loyal to you. Physicians, hospitals and other medical professionals often establish good relationships with vendors for various reasons. However, the complexities of medicine and the natural resistance to change can make unseating existing relationships difficult.

But, once you establish good relationships and maintain them properly, you will be allowed to fix situations that may arise and threaten to derail your business. This practice is critically important to the long-term success of your selling career. Converting business does not often happen overnight and the ability to recognize opportunities in advance is key. The wise medical sales professional is constantly on the lookout for such opportunities.

Professionalism

When selling in any industry, professionalism is a plus. When selling in the medical environment, it is an absolute requirement. You are selling to professionals, possibly some of the most highly educated and trained leaders in their field. These professionals have been entrusted with the sacred task of improving and maintaining patients' health.

Professional behavior in all aspects of medical sales is so critically important that if you have any doubts about your ability to be an absolute professional at all times, either commit to doing what it takes to become one, or do something else.

Education

Most candidates hired for medical sales have a bachelor's degree or higher, but not everyone in medical sales must have a college degree. Some of the highest-earning medical sales representatives that I know never went to college. But the applicant pool is mainly college-educated, so unless you want to work your way in through the "back door" (it can be successfully done), a college degree is almost essential.

One trait that does not necessarily come with a college degree, however, is a professional demeanor. You are selling to some of the most educated people in society, so good grammar and speaking skills are a must, along with other intangibles that are expected from an educated person. You must be perceived as knowledgeable, which is difficult if you cannot speak intelligently or write a coherent sentence.

The Money

Most people seek careers in medical sales because of the income potential, and believe me, it's there. But many beginning representatives focus too much on immediate income, instead of a long-term business plan. If you do the right things, at the right time, the money will come; focus on the money alone and your career is going to be short.

One problem for entrants into medical sales is trying to have too much too soon. Many medical representatives want all the trappings of success right away. I hired John for a junior sales position on a Friday afternoon. He was driving a seven-year-old Ford Escort and telling time with a black plastic sports watch. On Monday morning, John showed up for his first day of work driving a new BMW and wearing a brand-new Rolex.

"Nice car, John," I said. "Nice watch. Did you rob a bank?"

John replied, "I want to start out with the right image. The car is only $399 a month."

Part of me was a bit irritated that the "new kid" was going to be driving a $50,000 car to my accounts, wearing a $5,000 wrist watch. I couldn't hold back. I asked him, "John, did you get a good deal on the Rolex?"

He said, "Yeah, pretty good. It's only $219."

"$219? You mean it's not real? You bought a knockoff?"

Then, John lowered his eyes and his voice, and said, "$219 a month, for 36 months."

Don't get me wrong; I'm not opposed to owning nice things and rewarding oneself for a job well done. But wait until you've earned the success, or it can hurt your business—here's how. Doctors and hospital employees work very hard for their salaries and fees, and it often seems to them that someone is trying to reduce their income. It is one thing for these people to work with a sales representative and see him or her grow from a humble beginning to a true professional that the medical community considers a part of the team.

But, when a new, young rep walks in for the first time with such expensive trappings, it just might rub some of his customers the wrong way, especially if they look like they just graduated from college. Dealing with jealousy is a part of any type of success, but it can also prevent you from becoming successful in the first place. As one doctor customer told me, "When I see a kid who is barely old enough to shave, show up in my office acting like he's a hot-shot rich guy, I don't want to do business with him."

Does it mean that every prospect or customer is going to perceive John as this doctor did? No, but if you're just starting out in medical sales and you're in your early twenties, take it slow with the glitz until your customers have time to know and respect you. Believe me; no medical professional will be sold on your products because you paid more to know what time it is.

Work Environment

Depending on what products or services you sell, the work environment in medical sales can be more demanding than anything you ever imagined. This is especially true if you sell products that require you to service them or to be available to provide product expertise when they are used.

The medical professional doesn't want to hear about your company's backorders or delivery problems. When a product is needed, it's because a patient needs it now. The expectation is that you will deliver to the customer promptly or they will call someone else. Thus, you must take personal ownership of your company's backorder or delivery system in order to make things happen.

Medical sales can be a stressful field. Most people justify it because they enjoy the work and the paycheck that comes with it. Part of your success is learning how to prepare and execute duties so as to minimize the stress in your life. But, make no mistake, stress is a part of the package. You need to know how to deal with it or it will take its toll on your personal life and your health.

Everyone you work with in this field is under some level of pressure. Being responsible for people's lives is stressful and working with people who are stressed is going to create stress for you. One of the best ways to reduce your stress is to reduce theirs, by following through on what you've promised them.

Another element that creates stress is the need to juggle many tasks at once, so one of the best skills you can cultivate is good time management. I'm not talking about everything fitting neatly into a 9 to 5 schedule, but being able to adapt to a day that turns from a well-planned agenda into a 911 crisis.

Medical sales is not just about keeping your customer happy; you also need to keep your company happy, and the best way to do that is to grow your business. No matter how busy you are taking care of the customers, the status quo just doesn't cut it in sales. A salesperson's number one job is to bring in new business and grow the current business, all while maintaining the business you already have. It's a balancing act.

The Cost of Mistakes—Risk Management

The cost of sales mistakes in most businesses is a dollar amount. However, when you sell to healthcare professionals, a single mistake, an oversight or a lack of attention can cost a life. It can ruin the career of a physician or other healthcare provider and can cost everyone, including the sales representative, a lot of money.

Part of becoming a medical sales representative is the willingness to assume the risks that come with the job and to be competent at managing those risks. Things can and do happen that will keep you up at night or cause extreme stress. It is important to assess whether or not you have the ability to withstand working in an environment where risks like these must be managed at all times.

The Payoff

A bigger payoff than money for many people in medical sales is in knowing that they are contributing to improving the quality of people's lives. When you sell products that help people get better, live longer or save their lives, getting those products into the hands of the people who have the skills to use them is mission-critical. There is no better feeling than to have healthcare providers thank you, the salesperson, for helping them to provide better care to their patients and making a difference in patients' lives. Contributing to a positive outcome for a patient is a thrill of which you will never grow tired.

Clearly, there is a high income potential in medical sales that draws in many people, but there are also so many other rewards besides money that can't be obtained in any other type of sales career. Selling in medicine is different.

3

Why the Medical Sales Representative is a Professional

The definition of professional states that: *A professional performs an activity to receive payment for an act, which usually requires expertise and carries with it socially significant norms and customs.*

My mantra for medical sales is, **"Professionalism plus proficiency provides the payoff."** That sounds good rolling off the tongue, but what does it mean to be a professional?

It's a pretty broad definition, and yet it relates directly to occupations that most people think of as professional, such as doctors, lawyers and accountants. Considering the definition above, the medical sales professional definitely fits into this category.

The term "professional" is often regarded in a positive way. For example, "They live in a community of upscale professionals." Or, "I like that woman. She acts in a very professional manner."

Some people believe you can only be a professional if you hold a specific degree. No universities offer degrees in medical sales, so some might argue that medical sales is not truly a profession. I disagree. To be an effective medical sales representative, you must think of yourself as a professional, just as doctors and other healthcare professionals do.

In order to sell effectively in the medical world, you must believe that you personally bring something of value to the healthcare equation. Doctors and other professionals, as experts in their respective fields, can seem intimidating to salespeople who don't recognize their own value. Healthcare providers could not do their jobs without competent salespeople to educate them about products and services, make those products and services available, provide detailed product knowledge and provide service during and after the sale. In other words, as a medical sales professional, you are not inconsequential in your importance to patient care—you are an essential, supporting resource.

The Rules of Professionalism for Medical Sales

Rule number one: It's all about the patient.

There are several elements to be mindful of when you earn your living as a medical sales professional. You are essentially operating your own small business, so you need to be concerned with business issues. This means you have to maintain a schedule; operate efficiently to maximize profits; and deal with all of the logistical issues of a business, such as buying and maintaining business equipment, including a cell phone, computer, copier, fax machine, voice mail service, car, office space or home office, necessary attire, etc.

You also are responsible to the company or companies that you represent. They expect you to sell their products and comply with regulatory issues. Companies also set expectations for sales of product and services, something you probably know as quota. They also may require sales representatives to perform other tasks, such as surveys of customers and inventory control. With so much to do, it's sometimes easy to forget what healthcare is all about; the most important person in the healthcare system—the patient.

If there is a secret to successful medical sales, it is probably this: Structure your sales approach so that the spotlight is on improving patient outcomes. If you make what's best for the patient your number one priority, you'll always do the right thing and your customers will sense this. A patient-focused sales approach helps to keep the healthcare provider's attention on the patient. This avoids distraction by other influences, such as personal gain or loss and politics. Medical sales professionals who focus on the patient often achieve a level of professionalism above and beyond much of their competition. Work hard, work smart, focus on the patient and watch good things happen in your medical sales career.

Rule number two: You're In sales

Many medical sale representatives try to avoid the term, "salesperson." They'll use terms like technical representative, territory manager, marketing consultant, etc. Why is that?

For many, the word conjures up a negative connotation. Too often, the sales profession is seen as those who influence people to make bad buying decisions. Have you ever heard someone say, "That guy sounds like a used-car salesman?" I don't think that statement is ever meant as a compliment! We Americans often view salespeople as more of an unwanted interruption than as an essential provider of products and services.

You must make a decision: are you a provider of essential products and services to the healthcare industry, or are you an unwelcome interruption? By remembering rule number one and focusing on the patient, you will not be perceived in a negative way. But don't forget that you're in sales.

To be successful in medical sales means to demonstrate to the customer that your product and services are the right choice for that provider's patients, under the proper circumstances. You offer treatment options that are more advanced, more cost-effective, offer better results, have lower risks, etc. Your job is to make your customers aware of these options and to ask them to consider your proposal. This includes asking for the business when the time is appropriate. Remember, your customers know that you are in sales. They won't be shocked, dismayed, or disappointed when you ask them to consider using your product. It's what you do and they expect it. Don't wait for *them* to ask if they can try it or buy it. You're in sales, and it is your job to ask for the business!

Rule number three: You must be competent.

You must accept the fact that competency is a requirement, in terms of learning everything you need to know about your product and how it can benefit the patient and healthcare provider. You must be competent in imparting the appropriate knowledge to that healthcare provider. You must be competent in servicing and troubleshooting any issues related to your product or service. And lastly, but not least, you must be competent in selling your product. Competency is a requirement for all professional-level jobs, and medical sales is no exception.

It is vitally important that you acknowledge that medical sales is a professional occupation. If you are still not convinced that you are worthy of professional status, see if this syllogism helps:

- Doctors and other health care providers are professionals who offer care for their patients, employing the necessary knowledge and skills. They are paid accordingly.
- Medical sales representatives contribute to patient care by offering valued products and services to healthcare professionals and help-

ing them effectively use them by employing the necessary knowledge and skills. They are paid accordingly.

- Therefore, medical sales representatives are, by definition, professionals.

If you agree with this syllogism (and even if you don't), there should be no question in your mind that medical sales representatives are professionals. It is crucial that the healthcare providers you will be supporting must see you as a professional. The public that they serve expects nothing but professionalism from them; therefore, everyone with whom they work must be held to the same high standard. Should you not be regarded as a true professional, those healthcare professionals may refuse to do business with you. Therefore it is incumbent upon you to take every step necessary to ensure that you are considered a professional.

Merely calling yourself a professional, of course, does not make you one. Professionals earn that title by conforming to a high set of standards and expectations. Your customers—healthcare providers—are held to very high professional standards, not only by the various regulatory agencies, but by the public, as well. These customers will hold you to a high professional standard, too.

While it might seem rudimentary, let's make sure that we are on the same page when it comes to standards of professional behavior for medical sales professionals. Your impulse, at this point, may be to quickly gloss over these standards while you create the notion that you conform to each of them. *I implore you not to do this.* Go through the list, being as introspective as you can. Review each standard and ask yourself: Do I measure up? If not, what can I do or change to measure up?

Rule number four: You must observe standards of professional behavior

Standards of Professional Behavior for Medical Sales Professionals

1. **Integrity**—Integrity means being morally sound. It means you can be trusted and are of sound character. People with integrity are honest. Your customers can trust you with confidential information about their patients and their practice.

2. **Empathy**—Empathy is your ability to have compassion for the patient and the patient's family. Having empathy also means that you understand the healthcare provider's role in caring for patients and their families.

3. **Self-motivation**—Self-motivation is your ability to initiate learning about your products and services and continue to do so on a continuous basis and to stay current with the trends in your industry. It is also your ability to get out of bed every morning with a clearly defined purpose that drives you to do whatever needs to be done to effectively serve your customers and their patients. Self-motivation will empower you to honor the commitments that you have made to your customers without the need for someone to remind you.

4. **Appearance and personal hygiene**—You need to look the way a professional performing your job is expected to look. This includes, but is not limited to, maintaining appropriate clothing, a conservative hairstyle, and minimal, tasteful jewelry. You will also do well to avoid or cover tattoos and piercings. Your grooming will be seen as a reflection of your commitment to professionalism.

5. **Self-confidence**—It is critically important that you convey a strong degree of self-confidence; otherwise, your customers just won't have trust in you or what you are selling. Remember that they are making decisions that directly affect their patients. Would you gamble with your patient's life by working with a salesperson who doesn't appear to be very confident? No one wants to be treated by a doctor who lacks confidence in his or her clinical abilities. Similarly, you will find that healthcare professionals seek to do business with medical sales professionals that project confidence in their products or services and in themselves.

6. **Communications**—Professionals know how to speak clearly, write clearly and legibly, and effectively communicate their thoughts in a way that is easily understood. An important part of good communication is to be an active listener. The information that your customers provide you is what allows you to help them treat their patients with your products or services. You must be clear that you understand what they are saying and know how to communicate your understanding in a way that confirms it. Your customers also must be very clear at all times about what you are telling them.

7. **Time management**—Your job as a medical sales representative is essentially the same as running a small business, and your success will be determined to a large extent by your ability to effectively and efficiently manage your time. This is often overlooked by medical salespeople who leave their schedule to happenstance and the influence of others. You must arrive on time for any appointments with your customers or if circumstances prevent that, let them know immediately.

8. **Diplomacy**—Professionals know how to employ tact to gain a strategic advantage. Often, the first words that come into your mind when you are in a tense situation are not the best to use. Diplomacy is really the ability to think before speaking and knowing how to say something that will not offend or conflict with the other party's sensibilities.

9. **Team player**—The medical sales professional must often function as a part of a team, whether it is the team of medical professionals providing patient care or your own sales and support team. Some salespeople believe they can perform better as a "lone wolf" than as a team player, but lone wolves almost never do as well as those who take advantage of all of the resources and talent available. There are times when you must depend upon others to accomplish what needs to be done and times when others are depending upon you. You must both act and be perceived as a team player to maximize your success.

10. **Respect**—A medical sales professional is always polite to others, including his competitors; even to customers that are not always easy to work with. Speak only with respect about all your customers or say nothing at all. When you "badmouth" one customer to another, that customer may then wonder what you say about him or her to others. It is important not to use derogatory or demeaning language about anyone, ever. A word of advice is to never say anything about someone that you would not say if they were in the same room with you.

11. **Patient advocate**—The medical sales professional will always place the needs and the well-being of the patient above all else. This can be painful when the short-term potential to lose a sale is a consequence of doing the right thing. However, the price

for not doing the right thing will be longer lasting. Remember that *the patient comes first, no matter what.*

12. **Physician and healthcare provider advocate**—The medical sales professional will always act in a manner that demonstrates he or she has an understanding for and supports the needs and goals of the healthcare provider. That means that you won't sell a product or perform a service if there is a chance it could damage the physician or healthcare provider's professional reputation. This means placing your customer's needs ahead of your own, but never ahead of the patient's.

13. **Careful delivery of service**—The medical sales professional masters and maintains all the skills necessary to perform his or her job at the highest possible level. This includes thorough checks of all instruments, equipment and products and following policies, procedures and protocols consistent with best industry practices. With the patient as the ultimate beneficiary of your product or service, recognize the need to do everything to help the healthcare provider produce the optimal outcome.

14. **Honors the medical sales profession**—The medical sales professional will always act and behave in a way that brings credit to his or her profession. This means that you will never behave in a way that may cause customers to distrust you or other members of the medical sales profession. Always be realistic in terms of your capabilities and the limitations of your product or service.

If you are able to satisfy these 14 criteria, demonstrate a good work ethic and represent dependable products and services from reputable companies, you will likely succeed as a medical sales professional, earning the respect and income that goes along with it.

It's time now to see how you measure up by taking a realistic look at yourself. Please complete the professional assessment on the next page. For the rest of your medical sales career, prospects and customers will judge you by these criteria, whether you like it or not. Therefore, I am going to ask you to *be brutally honest with yourself as to how you rate in each category*. If you tend to be a little easy on yourself as you go through each item, please keep in mind that your customers may not be as kind. If you want some subjective feedback on how others see you, ask a close friend to honestly evaluate you on the criteria. Hopefully, you'll still be friends afterwards.

Competent professionals are generously rewarded in medical sales. Master these concepts and you are well on your way to a successful career.

Professional Behavior Evaluation
for the Medical Sales Professional

Integrity	☐ Competent	☐ Not Competent
Self-Motivation	☐ Competent	☐ Not Competent
Appearance and Personal Hygiene	☐ Competent	☐ Not Competent
Empathy	☐ Competent	☐ Not Competent
Communications	☐ Competent	☐ Not Competent
Team Player	☐ Competent	☐ Not Competent
Self-Confidence	☐ Competent	☐ Not Competent
Diplomacy	☐ Competent	☐ Not Competent
Respect	☐ Competent	☐ Not Competent
Time Management	☐ Competent	☐ Not Competent
Careful Delivery of Service	☐ Competent	☐ Not Competent
Patient Advocate	☐ Competent	☐ Not Competent

Advocate for the
Healthcare Provider ☐ Competent   ☐ Not Competent

Honors the Medical
Sales Profession   ☐ Competent   ☐ Not Competent

4

You Are a Professional—
Look the Part

People prefer to associate and engage in business with others that they perceive to be like themselves. I believe this is especially true in the interactions between medical professionals and salespeople. Because so much depends upon the buying decisions each healthcare provider makes, your customers may experience a subliminal sense of confidence if they see some of their own qualities reflected in you. Although a salesperson may in many ways be very different than the buyer, the buyer has their own perception of himself or herself. Let me give you an example.

Some orthopedic companies like to hire representatives who were involved with organized athletics in college and high school. There are many reasons for this, such as these former athletes are considered to be competitive, team players, and go-getters. There is also another reason. Many orthopedic surgeons are former athletes who remain very active in sports. Some of them are drawn to salespeople that have the qualities they would like to see in themselves—of being athletic and attractive. While this may not be the primary determining factor that an athletic orthopedic surgeon will use to make buying decisions, all things being equal, it could have an effect.

In medical sales, you sell to a variety of professionals—physicians, nurses, allied health professionals and health care administrators. These people all regard themselves as professionals, and as a consequence, are more confident buying from salespeople they consider to be professional. While it is critically important to behave professionally at all times, you must also look the part.

Dress like a Professional

"You never get a second chance to make a good first impression," is a quote worth remembering in the medical sales profession. But it's not only the first impression that's important, it's the ongoing perception. One thing that makes a consistent impact every time you're in front of a buyer is your grooming and dress.

There are different attitudes about dress in the medical sales profession. The goal is to be neither underdressed nor overdressed, so that your customers are comfortable with your appearance. Most sales reps have a fear of being underdressed, and tend to compensate by always being immaculately attired. In most situations, it is better to err on the side of being overdressed, but you need to be careful.

Early in my sales career, I acquired the Florida Keys as part of my territory. Wanting to make a good first impression, I dressed in my usual business attire, which was a dark suit, shirt and tie. I quickly learned that this attire was not appropriate for selling in the "Conch Republic." When I met the director of purchasing for one of the hospitals there, he was wearing a pair of shorts, a tropical shirt and a pair of rubber flip-flops. He appeared somewhat cautious and uncomfortable when he saw me walk into his office. Once I identified myself as a salesperson, he relaxed and the next words out of his mouth were, "I'm not even going to talk to you until you take off that jacket and remove your tie." I later learned that people who wore suits and ties in the Florida Keys usually held unwelcome positions in the federal government. I needed to dress down a bit to be perceived in a better light. From then on, for all of my sales trips to the Florida Keys, I wore khaki pants and a polo shirt with the company logo.

A good rule is to dress at least as well as your customer and at times, one notch higher, depending on the circumstances. For example, if you have a customer who is always wearing a business suit and he or she keeps the jacket on, you should do the same. If a male customer always wears a tie, you should wear a tie. A jacket is a good idea too, especially if the customer does not know you very well. If the situation calls for it, you can always take off your jacket, remove your tie and roll up your shirtsleeves. But there is little that you can do to dress up a polo shirt, a pair of scrubs or other forms of casual dress.

Dressing well for your customers is a sign of respect, and they will notice. I ran into Dr. Scott at a conference and stopped to ask him about Jim, who I had just hired a month earlier. Dr. Scott told me that Jim had stopped by his office earlier that week to introduce himself, so I asked the doctor his impression of Jim. Dr. Scott said, "He seems like a nice kid (Jim was in his mid-twenties and Dr. Scott in his early sixties), but I'm a little surprised that he would show up for our first meeting without a tie. In fact, he was wearing scrubs!" Dr. Scott's smile could not hide the irritation. He always wore a suit with a shirt and tie and that jacket never came off. Jim had not made a good first impression.

Medical sales representatives who sell surgical equipment, implants and supplies may spend part of their day dressed in surgical scrubs. While this is appropriate for servicing the customer in the operating room and other departments in a hospital or clinic, it is not appropriate for a sales call with a health care professional unless you need to be in scrubs to enter the location where you will be calling on that person. Jim may have thought, "I'm going to be going in and out of hospitals today, and I don't feel like wearing a suit. Dr. Scott, as a surgeon, will understand why I'm dressed in scrubs—he knows what I do." Dr. Scott knew why Jim was in scrubs, but still couldn't understand why Jim didn't care enough to be dressed more appropriately for their first meeting.

Know what is considered appropriate attire for selling in your territory. Your company may dictate your mode of address, and if so, I advise you to follow their instructions to the letter. If you regularly violate the dress code, the company will learn of it and it won't be good for your career.

If you wear a suit, make sure it fits well. Suits that are too short, too long, too large or too tight are obviously ill-fitting. Make sure your suit, shirt and tie coordinate. Shoes should be shined and in good repair (i.e., no worn heels or holes in the soles).

I gave you an example of how being overdressed when I was selling in the Florida Keys had a negative impact. Here is another example that I have personally witnessed several times. Most of my career was engaged in surgical sales. I spent much of my time in operating rooms throughout my territory, and I learned a few things about how some O.R. personnel regard salespeople. This is one scenario that played out over and over, with respect to salespeople's dress.

Men and women who work in the operating room don't look very glamorous when they are doing their jobs. As you probably know, they wear surgical scrub clothes that don't have much style or design, everyone's hair must be covered with an unflattering cap, jewelry is discouraged, nails must be clipped short and fingernail polish is often not allowed. Many women forego makeup and some men don't bother to shave. Everyone is there to do his or her job the best they can, but the truth is that O.R. personnel do not look their best when they are at work!

Here is an example of a well-dressed female sales representative getting a negative response to her appearance. I have seen it occur more than once, but this particular event stayed with me. Several female O.R. staff members were in the O.R. lounge waiting to meet with a salesperson I'll call Betty. The staff, as usual, are wearing surgical scrubs, hats, no makeup and sneakers or unflattering O.R.-type shoes that are stained with various prep solutions and bodily fluids. All are somewhat tired from a full morning of surgical cases.

Betty enters the lounge for her appointment. She's wearing a well-tailored designer dress, stockings and expensive, high-heeled shoes. Her hair and makeup are perfect. The scent of her perfume can be detected throughout the lounge and even in the hallway of the O.R. She's wearing beautiful, expensive jewelry, many pieces of which contain diamonds, and an expensive watch. The gaudy keychain with the BMW insignia that she is holding is making an impression, as well. Several of the doctors and the male staff are gathering outside the room to admire "the visitor." One of the men compliments Betty on how nice she looks. Betty certainly stands out in a room of O.R. professionals who are only dressed for work.

Do you remember that I said that people prefer to associate with and engage in business with those that they perceive to be like themselves? I could see that some of the staff clearly identified with Betty's attractive and well-dressed appearance, but most of the ladies felt uncomfortable around her. One of the nurses remarked to Betty, "It must be really nice to be able to dress like a woman for work." The nurse wasn't smiling.

When Betty finished her presentation, one of the other ladies who had been present said, "Well she doesn't look like she's hurting! I don't think she really needs our business." A few of the ladies chuckled, and the rest walked out. But it was clear that some of the women at the meeting took a dislike to Betty because they felt like she was flaunting her femininity, with clothing and accessories that they could not wear, and some probably could not afford. It seemed that Betty's appearance worked against her, at least with that group.

Several days later, at the same hospital, a sales rep named Jane came in to meet with the same group. Jane used to be a nurse, so she probably bonded with many of the nurses in the O.R. just because of that, but Jane displayed no sense of style. Her clothes were usually wrinkled (not very different from the scrubs the O.R. staff were wearing), her hair was often windblown or uncombed and she never wore jewelry or nail polish. In short, she dressed in a way that did not create jealousy or resentment.

The message is to develop a feel for your customers and dress accordingly. It is better to err on the side of being a little overdressed, as opposed to underdressed, but don't overdo either one.

Proper dress includes not overdoing things like jewelry and other signs of success. Many of us like luxury cars and expensive watches, but the fact is that some of your customers are going to be put off if you're wearing a $15,000 Rolex President watch and driving a Mercedes. I'm not saying you should or shouldn't own these luxury items. Just consider the fact that some of your customers may resent you for it and may not buy from you as a result.

Grooming and Hygiene

Unfortunately, it is necessary to address these habits in a book targeted at professional salespeople. Despite the myriad soaps, deodorants, shampoos, toothpastes, mouthwashes and hair trimmers on the market, still too many sales professionals maintain inadequate practices in the grooming department. Too often I have encountered medical salespeople with body odor, bad breath and long nose hairs. These are things you don't want your customers to remember you by.

Don't eat onions for lunch if you have a sales presentation to follow. If you must consume aromatic foods, take the time to brush your teeth or rinse with mouthwash or use a breath spray. Check to make sure you don't have a piece of spinach stuck between your front teeth.

If you smoke, quit. Most medical professionals who once smoked have given it up. Smokers have offensive breath—breath mints do little for the smell coming out of your lungs, and the hair and clothing of smokers gives them away. It's a turn-off, and many health care providers prefer to not be around smokers.

If you have dandruff, consider not wearing dark-colored jackets, shirts or blouses. Check and brush your shoulders off before you meet with customers, not during the meeting! Think about getting help from a dermatologist, who may be able to help you manage or eradicate the condition.

Hair should always be neatly cut and styled. Gentlemen, the hair that grows on your neck needs to be shaved between haircuts—you can't see it, but everyone else can. Shave every day. Beards are acceptable if they are neatly trimmed, but understand that if you sell products used in the operating room and you need to be present during surgeries from time to time, some doctors don't like beards from a bacterial standpoint. If you're trying to land a big customer, you might want to find out how he or she feels about beards and groom accordingly.

Tattoos and Body Jewelry

My company had a fellow working for us named Jim in the late 1990s. His job was to deliver surgical instruments and implants to operating rooms and to set them up. Jim showed up to work one Monday morning with a large, bright tattoo of a tiger on the back of his neck! When I arrived in the operating room that morning, one of the nurses took me aside and told me that one of the patients in the holding area saw Jim's tattoo and commented that it was "ugly and inappropriate" for a doctor. Of course, Jim was not a doctor, but to a patient in the hospital, any person walking around in scrubs might be involved in his or her care, and if that person does not look professional or competent to them, it creates concern. The nurse suggested that I talk to Jim about covering the tattoo when he came into the hospital. She said, "It does not look professional."

Staff members in other hospitals made negative comments about Jim's tattoo, as well. Unfortunately, Jim had not considered the implications of a tattoo on an exposed part of his body. He was offered the option of removing it or resigning, and chose the latter.

Tattoos may be in vogue as acceptable works of art, but in my experience, many in the medical profession do not view tattoos in such a positive light. Some tattoos can be covered by clothing if they are strategically located, so keep this in mind if you're considering some new body art.

Earrings are acceptable for women if they are conservative and in good taste. Men may even get by with them on occasion, but medicine is a conservative community, with conservative values. It comes down to how your management and your customers feel about men wearing earrings. The good news is that earrings can be removed. Body piercing such as eyebrow rings, lip rings, and tongue studs will not likely be viewed by the medical community as professional attire. Leave them at home.

Don't forget that your appearance creates the first impression your customers will have of you. Do your best to make it a good one.

5

Everything You Do Matters

Congratulations—you're a medical sales professional! As the result of everything you have done up until this point, you are developing rich and lasting relationships with your customers that make you an integral part of the patient care team. Your customers see you not only as a vendor and resource, but also as a trusted friend. Now, the future of your business and business relationships depends upon everything you do—*everything!* In business–especially *this* business–everything you do matters.

When I say everything matters, I'm not talking about only what you do when you have your business suit on or when you're actively working with a customer. I'm referring to everything in your life. What you do in your personal life, and even your private life, can have a huge impact on your business should it become known to your customers. The friends you keep, the organizations to which you belong, the establishments you frequent, your habits, where you live and how you keep your home and property and the person you date or are married to, can all affect your business success.

You may be saying, "Well, that's not fair—what I do outside of work is my business!" That may be true from a legal perspective, but anything you do that affects how your customers feel about you and how they feel about their association with you can influence their decision to do business with you or not.

You Never Know When You Will Run Into a Customer

If you are new to the business or to your territory, the chances are that you have not even met all of your customers yet. You would hate to meet one the way this sales rep did.

Ted, a representative who sold products to the OB/GYN community, stopped at a take-out restaurant on his way home from work. Ted had been in the territory for about six weeks and was still in the phase of working his way around to meet all of his customers. While he was in line to place his order at the restaurant, a man who was at the front of the line began shouting abusively at one of the female employees. When Ted looked over, he noticed that the young girl was crying as the man berated her with obscenities and threats. Ted, ever the gentleman (and a former college linebacker) felt the need to intervene and get the angry man to calm down. Ted said, "Sir, she's a young girl who's just trying to do her job. You don't have to speak to her that way. I think you need to stop." The irate man knew better than to initiate a physical confrontation with Ted, who was much bigger and many years younger than he. Yet, he couldn't resist stopping to shout some choice obscenities at Ted as he was walking past.

Ted stepped out of line and placed his face inches from the man's and said, "I don't know who the hell you think you're talking to but, you're just seconds away from getting seriously hurt." The man shouted one last obscenity and quickly left the restaurant. The ugly confrontation was over and Ted was glad that he kept his temper under control. He thought to himself, "I hope I never see that jerk again." Unfortunately, that was not to be.

A few weeks after the incident, Ted had an appointment to meet Dr. Edward Lee, the OB/GYN department chief at his largest account. Ted had been waiting for almost two months for the opportunity to introduce himself. Getting to know Dr. Lee was critically important, as the doctor influenced nearly every buying decision in his department.

Ted was well prepared for the meeting. Dr. Lee's secretary had scheduled 15 minutes (a generous amount of time for a busy department head) and Ted planned on using it efficiently to learn as much as he could about Dr. Lee's practice and the needs of the department in general. The receptionist escorted Ted into to the office of Dr. Lee, whose back was turned as he talked on the phone. As Dr. Lee turned in his chair, both men recognized each other at about the same time. When Ted realized that Dr. Lee was the man that he confronted at the restaurant a few weeks earlier, his stomach knotted in a way he will never forget. But he did not get much time to think about that, because Dr. Lee screamed, "What the hell are you doing here? Get the (bleep) out of my office. Barbara, call security." Poor Ted quickly exited the building.

He stayed with the company for a few more months, but Ted never tried to explain how he "threatened to hurt" one of his biggest customers. An unfortunate set of circumstances had placed Ted in a situation—albeit, an extreme one—in which doing the right thing can harm your business or cost you your job.

Your Personal and Private Life
Can Affect Your Business

Even what you do in your private life can have a drastic effect on your business. Alex, an orthopedic sales representative, ran a successful territory by day, but his personal life involved an alternative lifestyle. One evening, as he was dancing on the bar in his underwear at a nightclub in a resort city 100 miles from home, two nurses from one of his biggest accounts walked into the club out of curiosity. They just could not believe their eyes when they saw Alex—a professional, successful, highly regarded medical sales professional, dancing almost naked in a severely intoxicated state in an atmosphere where no one would have ever expected to find him. They also could not resist telling everybody in the operating room about what they had witnessed!

Medical sales professionals often have close business and sometimes, personal relationships with their customers. All are to some degree judged by the people they associate with. Healthcare professionals must protect their reputations to maintain the trust of their colleagues and patients. In many ways, when a healthcare professional enters into a business relationship with you, he is saying that he trusts your character enough to be associated with you.

Alex had unknowingly burned his bridges. Orthopedics is a male-dominated, macho specialty. Once word of Alex's escapade made its way around the operating room and the hospital, many of the orthopedists began to move their business to other companies. Was this an unfair form of discrimination that could be challenged in a court of law? Maybe, but when all was said and done, the business was gone. Bill didn't realize that, "Everything you do matters."

You might think that Alex had some options to recover the business. Maybe he could just talk to his customers or threaten a lawsuit.

How many of the customers do you think would confess to moving their business because of Alex's after-hours activities? Could Alex ever prove that the reason he lost business is because of the way he lived his life after work? How would it affect his business relationships if he openly confronted his customers regarding their feelings about his personal life? And finally, if he decided to file any lawsuits based on this presumption, do you think that anyone would ever do business with him again?

I did not share this story to tell you how you should or should not live your life, nor I am condoning or condemning any lifestyle choices. I am pointing out that, while you have the legal right to live your life anyway that you wish, doing so may still harm your business.

Everything you do matters.

Relationships

Your success in medical sales will in some part be based on your ability to develop and maintain good relationships. Let's look at the different relationship levels and how each might affect your business.

The Basic Business Relationship

A basic business relationship is what you will have with most of your customers. This is one in which you interact with your customers only as it relates to business, and little else. The relationship is predicated on the customer's belief in your products and services and that you will do what you say you're going to do, as your company's representative. Generally, these relationships cause few problems, as long as nothing is done to violate the customer's trust or expectations.

There is not much that can go wrong with the basic business relationship, but it still happens. For example, I was always very straight-laced in my business dealings and my personal life, so I was very shocked when I received a call one day from Dr. Clinton, who said he was ready to switch suppliers and demanded a meeting.

I met with the doctor. He informed me that he just learned that Dr. Jones across town was using the same surgical device I provided to him. Dr. Clinton did not care for Dr. Jones and further stated that if Dr. Jones was using my product, he would stop using it, because Dr. Jones made the product "look bad." I had to inform Dr. Clinton that there was nothing that I could do to keep Dr. Jones from using my product—he had the necessary credentials and it was neither in my power, nor in my company's interest, to deny him. Dr. Clinton switched to a competitive product and that took a large chunk out of my commission check. What had I done wrong? Nothing! Dr. Clinton's ego and dislike for Dr. Jones led him to make an irrational decision. Within a few months, Dr. Clinton returned to using my product after having less than satisfactory results with a competitor's product, but I was always waiting for his next phone call. Some of your business relationships will be rocky, due to circumstances you cannot control. You just do the best you can, try to keep your customers happy and continue to grow your business.

Let me add that sometimes, when your customers won't buy from you, there may be underlying reasons like the one I described with Dr. Clinton, but your customers won't always be as forthcoming. Keep in mind that when a customer isn't buying, there could be some underlying motivation that you have not considered.

The Friendship Business Relationship

It is wonderful to develop true friendships during the course of business. Friendships can take what is normally considered work and turn it into an ongoing, enjoyable experience. Friendships bring many benefits, but also present a few potential pitfalls. You must be wary about how friendships can affect your business.

The Good

Friendships are good because people like doing business with other people that they know, like, and trust, and friendship cannot exist without those three elements. The benefits of a business relationship with a friend are numerous, starting with adding a dimension of pleasure to business that is not found elsewhere. It's great to be able to work with people that you enjoy spending time with when you're not working.

One of the obvious perceived benefits of friendship in business is that it tends to solidify the selling relationship. Your friends will try to steer business your way, as long as it is in the best interest of their patients. Friends will keep you informed about what is happening in their practices and institutions as it pertains to your business. If they become aware of anything that threatens your business, they will often notify you, so that you are not caught off-guard by the information. Your friends are usually eager to recommend you and your products and services to other medical professionals, which gives you credibility and helps to drive your business. Your customer-friends may be more understanding of any product or service problems and will generally provide you with ample opportunities to correct them.

The Bad

You need to be aware also of the potential problems with business friendships.

One problem is, if your business is built more on the friendship than on the merits of your products and services, any change in the friend-ship will create a change in the business. This means that if you have a falling out or stop spending "friend time" with a customer, it could cost you the business. This is one reason why it is so critical not to cre-ate false friendships just for the purpose of generating business.

I called on Dr. Petersen, for years. He was a busy surgeon whose practice produced a large volume of business. Shortly after he began using my products, he asked me if I wanted to play golf with him on his day off. I told him that I was not a golfer, but he said, "Don't worry about it. You're going golfing with me. I'll teach you. Besides, I'm a good customer," he added with a smile. That was enough to sell me on the idea!

Spending half a day with Dr. Petersen playing golf was pleasant enough, but it also reminded me why I don't golf—I just don't enjoy the game. When we were having lunch in the clubhouse after 18 long holes, he said, "Mace, you need to do this on a regular basis if you're going to get good at it. Let's see about getting you a membership at the club."

I said, "Carl, membership would be a waste for me. It will probably be a long time until I play again."

Dr. Petersen interjected, "Nonsense. I know when you're playing again. You're playing again next Wednesday, with me."

I reminded Dr. Petersen that this was not *my* day off. "Carl, I might have some surgeries next Wednesday that I need to cover. I'll get back to you," I replied, with the full intention of getting out of another gru-eling attempt at golf.

"Get someone else to cover those surgeries. Just tell the boss that you're "working" with one of your best customers," Dr. Petersen added, with a look of expectation.

I struggled through 18 more holes of golf the following week with Dr. Petersen, but in the end, I was honest with him. I said, "Carl, I enjoy spending time with you, but I'm not a golfer. Listen, I would rather have dinner with you and your wife. I would find it more enjoyable. I know you eat and sleep golf, but for me, it's like going to the dentist."

Dr. Petersen said, "I'm disappointed, but okay—let's have dinner Friday night."

Friday night arrived. My wife and I enjoyed a somewhat pleasant meal dining with Dr. Petersen and his wife. Most of the evening was dominated by Dr. Petersen's conversation, telling us what a great surgeon he is and his belief that most of the other surgeons in town don't compare to his level of training and skill.

When the dinner was over and we were saying goodnight with the usual pleasantries, Dr. Petersen exclaimed, "We like you guys. Let's have a standing dinner date every Friday evening!"

I could see the color change in my wife's face. She does not enjoy spending time with self-centered people, and although she was willing to do it on occasion for me, I knew there was no way she would consent to spending time with Dr. Petersen on a regular basis. She quickly jumped in, "We're sorry; we already have plans for next Friday. Another time."

Dr. Petersen responded instantaneously, "What about Saturday or Sunday evening?"

"We have plans for the entire weekend," I said. "We'll do it again soon."

Over the next several weeks, Dr. Petersen pushed to try and get me to golf with him, dine with him and his wife (which we did again, reluctantly), but apparently, it wasn't enough. I noticed one of my competitors spending time at Dr. Petersen's office when I called on him, and they were talking dinner and golf. Within a month, the doctor was using all of my competitor's products and none of mine.

I talked to other sales reps who had worked with Dr. Petersen over the years. It turns out that this is how he operated—leveraging his business into "friendships." What Dr. Petersen wanted more than a good company with good products for his patients was "a friend."

Many medical sales professionals maintain bona fide friendships with their customers. I enjoyed close relationships with several of my customers over the years, but it was by mutual consent—not forced by me or the customer. Now, some of you may be saying, "Mace, you should have continued the friendship for the business." I thought about it, but the truth is that you can't make a relationship into more than what it really is. Sooner or later, either you or the customer will realize that the relationship is not real and it will end, and it could tarnish your reputation in the process. Business friendships are great, but only if they are based on genuine feelings, and not used as just a tool to get or sustain business

Truth About Doing Business with Friends

Some sales reps make the mistake of believing that their customer-friends don't expect the same level of service as their regular customers. Think of any interactions with your friends. Do you expect more from your friends in any situation or less? Here is the real truth about doing business with friends and please don't ever forget it:

Your customer-friends expect more from you in a business relationship, not less.

One of my best customers, Dr. Cohen, became a close friend. I enjoyed attending his surgeries when he was using my products and he enjoyed it as well, because with me, he knew he always had competent representation in his operating room. As I grew my territory, scheduling conflicts evolved where I needed to spend time with other surgeons instead of Dr. Cohen. Because he was a friend, I rationalized that he wanted me to be successful and earn more commissions. I told myself, "He'll understand." I spoke to Dr. Cohen and assured him that I would have my capable assistant Joe cover his surgeries.

The first surgery Joe covered did not go so well. Joe forgot to bring some critical instruments that made the operation more difficult for Dr. Cohen. When I was notified, I felt sick to my stomach and rushed to the hospital to apologize to Dr. Cohen in person. I assured him that Joe had learned his lesson and that it would never happen again. Unfortunately, later that same week, it did.

I was 1½ hours away, working with another surgeon, when I got the call from Joe, who was working with Dr. Cohen. He had given Dr. Cohen the wrong information regarding one of the products and the product became damaged in the process and could not be used. Joe needed to order another one from the warehouse, which prolonged the surgery by more than an hour. One of the staff nurses called to inform me that Dr. Cohen was fuming mad and that I had better get over there.

When the surgery that I was covering was finished, I rushed the 90 miles to fix things with my friend, Dr. Cohen. I thought I could easily smooth things over, as I had previously. I was wrong. When I greeted him in the hospital, he was so angry he would not look me in the eye. He just said, "Mace, come with me," as he hurriedly walked down the hallway. He opened the door to the operating room director's office and asked her if we could use her office for a few minutes, and she stepped out.

He said, "Mace, sit down. I want you to know that right now I'm talking to you as Dr. Cohen, the surgeon who uses your products—not as your friend, Steve. When I'm in the operating room, my first concern is my patient. I use your products because I get good results and because of the good service you have given me. I know I'm one of your best customers, but this week you haven't treated me like one of your best customers. I enjoy our friendship, but when I'm in the O.R., I'm not your friend—I'm a surgeon. How are you going to fix this?"

I felt sick to my stomach. Not only had I jeopardized the business with one of my best customers, I also disappointed a friend—something that made me feel far worse. I said, "Steve, I promise to treat you from now on like one of my best customers, because you are. I understand that if I can't give you the highest level of service, you'll take your business somewhere else, and you will be justified in doing so."

For the next 17 years, I treated Dr. Cohen as a customer first, and still enjoyed a wonderful friendship with him. We never had another problem.

Remember that any customers who think of you as a friend will expect more from you, not less. Some may even expect preferential treatment, which you may or may not be able to provide. Increased expectations are part of the friendship package.

If a Customer *Thinks* You're a Friend, Beware of What They Might Expect

In medical sales, one often works closely with the same customers, day-in and day-out. Frequently, there is a "feeling" of friendship even though you may not have socialized or taken the relationship beyond the work environment. Even this can get sticky under the wrong circumstances.

Many of the nurses and surgical technologists I worked with in the operating room expressed an interest in coming to work for me if I ever had any openings. Whenever a position opened up, like any sensible businessman, I opted to fill it with the person who was most capable of performing the job. To be honest, if a person was a friend, that was a good reason not to hire him or her. It was hard enough to manage people in often stressful situations. I did not want to have to manage a friend, because I knew either the friendship or the work relationship would suffer—probably, both. As a result, I would never openly solicit job candidates in any of my accounts, but would approach any qualified candidates discreetly.

It always created bad feelings when some of my customer-friends would learn that I hired someone without ever talking to them. It often changed the way they acted towards me, and a few times, these "friends" tried to punish me by taking away business. The vast majority of the times, friendships were beneficial, but every now and then they were just the opposite.

Friendships can also create problems if other employees in your accounts or even your competitors make accusations that you are getting preferential treatment and business opportunities because of the friendship. This may be construed as (and may be) a conflict of interest that can harm your business and reputation and get your friend in trouble or fired. Be very careful of situations where it is obvious that business is coming your way because of a friendship.

A friendship with one customer can create jealous feelings with another. Many people work in the medical environment, and not everyone likes each other. Unfortunately, some customers may try to punish you for being friends with someone they dislike by denying you business. There is not much that you can do about it, other than to be aware and attempt to minimize any harm by not discussing your friendships with other customers.

The Ugly

Some relationships can go bad in a big way and really cause you a lot of grief, from a business perspective. It's been said that you can judge a person by the friends that he or she keeps. Like it or not, your customers will be making judgments about you based on who your friends are and the people with whom you surround yourself.

Early in my career, a surgeon who had been one of my closest friends in childhood moved into my territory. We reestablished our friendship and over time, he became one of my best customers. My wife and I spent a large part of our spare time with him and his wife—we dined together, played tennis, fished and traveled together for many years. Our friendship was known to both my competitors and to many of the other physicians in the community.

Everything was great, until some of my friend's patients filed charges against him for misconduct. My friend denied the accusations. As word of this circled the community, I vehemently defended my friend, who had a stellar reputation as an excellent surgeon and a good person. Unfortunately, many more patients came forward and filed charges and my friend was arrested and pleaded no contest to the charges. He was asked to leave his practice and privileges at several hospitals were revoked. I was devastated that my friend had been lying to me regarding his involvement, and our friendship was irretrievably damaged. But I was unprepared for what I was about to personally experience in my business.

There were a few doctors and hospital employees who could not resist the opportunity to confront me what my friend had done. There was almost a suggestion of, "you had to know," despite the fact that I didn't have a clue and believed my friend's denials until he pleaded no contest. Some customers actually behaved differently toward me. One surgeon I did a lot of business with moved his business to another company. He had a huge dislike for my friend and told me, point-blank, "If you can be friends with a guy who did what he did, then as far as I'm concerned, you're just as bad as he is!"

The negative association quickly faded. I went about business in my territory as I always did, and a few months later, even the surgeon who accused me of being "just as bad" apologized and returned all of his business. The relationship with my friend went wrong when he went wrong, and for a while it did affect my business. This story serves as just another example of how everything you do matters.

The Romantic Business Relationship

If you have watched hospital soap operas over the years, some of what you have seen on TV happens in real life. The medical environment involves very intimate working conditions. Dealing with stress, working long days and spending hours in life-or-death situations creates strong bonds. Sometimes, romantic feelings evolve and can cause trouble.

The first thing to understand about romantic business relationships is that no one is immune. I can hear what some of you are saying— "I'm a married man," or "I'm a married woman." "I'm in a relation-ship—I'm not going to become romantically involved with any of my customers." Your intentions are honorable and you may, in fact, hold an unyielding commitment to that belief. Just beware that the romantic interest does not have to be yours for problems to occur. One of your customers may become attracted to you, and that can place your business in jeopardy.

If you are a medical sales professional with above average good looks, extraordinary charisma, or even just a pulse—then you are at risk—regardless of your marital or relationship status, or even your sexual orientation. I'm talking about a customer who tries to entice you into a romantic relationship. Trust me, it can happen. It happened to me.

When I was new in medical sales, one of my customers would not give me time to discuss a product that I was trying to sell unless I took her to lunch on her day off. I agreed, and because she was at least 20 years older than I was, the thought of her "coming on" to me never occurred.

During lunch, when I attempted to discuss my product with her, she insisted that she would only have that discussion at her house. She further informed me that her husband was out of town for the next few days, so no one would interfere with our "discussions." To make a long story short, I declined, she ordered the product from another company and punished me by refusing to meet with me ever again.

As human beings, there is always a possibility that we may find ourselves attracted to others in some way. Many of the professionals that medical sales professionals sell to are nice-looking and charismatic people. Finding yourself attracted to a customer is not a problem, unless you act on that attraction. You may not have any control over your feelings, but you can control whether or not you give in to those feelings. Recognize that any romantic involvement with professionals or other employees in your accounts is potentially dangerous to your business.

What happens if you are single and interested in a romantic relationship with a customer? Let's make this simple. In a romantic business relationship with a customer, as long as the relationship is fine, then the business part is fine. But should the relationship turn sour, you might be kissing your business good-bye.

Ben, a suture representative that I used to know, was hired into a territory that included a hospital account with more than $1 million worth of base business. Ben was a tall, handsome, 25 year-old man, who looked like he just walked out of the pages of GQ magazine. It was painful to watch the way women in the operating room would stop whatever they were doing and stare at Ben whenever he entered a room. Sara, the O.R. director, who was about 20 years older than Ben, recently divorced and extremely attractive, told Ben that it would be a good idea if they got to know each other better because of the high level of business Ben's company had with the hospital. To make a long story short, Sarah and Ben's relationship quickly escalated to intimacy, and while Ben perceived it as a fun time for the moment, Sarah was developing real feelings for him and wanted a serious relationship. When she told Ben about her feelings, Ben pointed out that he wanted to have children and due to her age and the fact that she already had raised children, she wasn't right for him.

It's been said (by William Congreve) that, "Hell hath no fury like a woman scorned." Sara immediately terminated the relationship with Ben and started making his life difficult when it came to doing business in her operating room. When Ben complained to the surgeons at the hospital that Sarah was taking out her anger on Ben's business, many of the surgeons, who liked and respected Sara, let her know that they were not happy with the gossip Ben was spreading about her. In less than two months, Ben's business at this hospital, which represented more than $1 million to his company, was zero.

There is no question that Ben made some bad mistakes, but the biggest was to become intimately involved with one of his customers, when he should have known that there would not be an opportunity for a graceful exit. Ben's story is only one of many that I can share with you. In fact, I could write a book just on this topic, and maybe one day, I will. We all know the joys of romance, but when it is mixed with business, it's like smoking a cigarette in a room full of gunpowder—you might survive it and then again, you might not.

Other problems are possible when one enters into a romantic relationship with a customer. These include:

- Management will be concerned that the judgment of the person with whom you are involved will be influenced by the relationship and affect their objective buying decisions. This places that employee in a potentially adversarial position with his or her employer.

- Your competitors will look to portray your relationship as giving you an unfair advantage in that account. Some of your customers may choose to support your competitor, based on this information.

- It may poison your relationships with other staff members who don't like the person with whom you are romantically involved.

- You will lose credibility with anything that person says about you or your products. For example, if you're dating Bob, who is the materials coordinator for the emergency room, and Bob suggests to the ER doctors that they should use your products because they are great, they may think, "Of course Bob is going to say that—he's dating Mary."

- If and when the relationship ends, more often than not, it creates uncomfortable working conditions, and if that person is looking to avoid you, he or she may do so by trying to get the account to avoid your products or services.

Flirtatious Behavior

Flirtatious behavior, in many ways, is part of human nature, but sexual harassment is a gigantic issue for all companies and institutions. Salespeople may flirt just to flatter a customer, bur regardless of the intent, this behavior is very dangerous and can easily be interpreted as harassment. Any time you decide to cross this line, even with what you perceive to be harmless, flirtatious behavior, you are endangering your career and placing yourself at risk for an expensive lawsuit.

Even just touching someone in a seemingly innocent way, by placing your hand on a shoulder, can be legitimately reported as sexual harassment. Ninety-nine times out of 100, nothing will happen when you touch someone in an appropriate way in the workplace, but the one time that it does can get very ugly. Just be aware.

Organizations

Any group, club, or organization that you belong to can affect your business in either a positive or negative way.

Being involved with reputable service organizations, such as Kiwanis or Rotary, can have a positive impact on your business, as it demonstrates that you are committed to service in the community. However, do not join one of these organizations solely for the purpose of benefiting your business, because people will sense it. Your purpose in joining must be because you strongly believe in the organization and its mission.

Joining organizations with a controversial agenda can impact your business. An example might be one that supports either pro-life or pro-choice with regard to abortion. People are divided on this issue, and for some, their feelings are passionate. Just seeing you in a picket line supporting one side or the other could be all that it takes for one of your healthcare customers to abandon doing business with you. Am I saying that you should abandon your beliefs for the sake of maintaining business? No, I'm just asking you to consider the ramifications of everything that you do, because everything you do matters.

Everything You Do Matters

In this chapter, I have given you examples of how seemingly harmless behavior can have a huge impact on your business. Since *everything* you do matters, and I don't have time here to discuss *everything,* it is your responsibility to consider the relationships and actions in your life and assess whether or not your business can be affected. I'm serious—you need to give this some thought. Years of hard work in your territory can be wiped out by a lack of forethought or just being in the wrong place at the wrong time.

Always assess the possibilities and probabilities that may result from your choices and consider the best-case scenario versus the worst-case scenario. If you are making good decisions the majority of the time, you will succeed

Everything you do matters.

6

Ethics and Personal Integrity in Medical Sales

I like to give people the benefit of the doubt when it comes to ethics and personal integrity. Selling in the medical environment requires a very high level of these traits. People might not always be watching, but you have the unspoken trust of the patient and the healthcare providers, expecting you to do the right thing at all times.

Selling, by definition, is about getting the order or making the sale. If you're not closing business, you're probably not eating very well. But sometimes in medical sales, you're in a position to close a deal and it's not the right thing to do, because your product or service is not right for the patient. Some medical sales reps defend moving ahead with the sale by rationalizing that it is the healthcare providers' decision regarding what products and services they use to treat their patients. This is true, and indeed a sound reason, but only if the healthcare provider has received full disclosure regarding all the implications of using your products or services. I call this the, "get the business versus do what is right conundrum." Let me give you an example.

Let's say that Bob, a medical sales professional, sells orthopedic implants. He is giving a sales presentation on his company's new hip prosthesis to Dr. Jones. Dr. Jones likes the hip prosthesis and wants to use it on a patient who weighs close to 400 pounds. Bob knows this particular hip prosthesis is contraindicated (should not be used) in patients over 350 pounds, because of the possibility of the prosthesis breaking, but he has been trying to get Dr. Jones to try his company's products for more than a year, and Bob stands to make a nice commission on the sale. What are Bob's options?

1. Bob can assume that Dr. Jones, as an experienced orthopedic surgeon, is aware of the potential risk of hip prosthesis failure in a heavy patient and not say anything. Bob has never even heard of one of his company's hip prostheses breaking in a patient. Bob doesn't apprise Dr. Jones of the potential risk.

2. Bob can be vague, asking questions such as, "Dr. Jones, do you have any concerns about doing a hip replacement on such a large patient?" If the doctor doesn't say that he is worried about the prosthesis breaking, then Bob rationalizes that the doctor has no concerns regarding potential prosthesis failure in a large patient.

3. Bob points out the contraindications in the product literature to Dr. Jones regarding the weight limitations for patients over 350 pounds. There is a chance that Dr. Jones might decide not to use Bob's product and call a competitor instead. There is also a chance that Dr. Jones may decide that the potential benefit outweighs the potential risk and go ahead with the operation using Bob's product.

What would you do? If you follow your company's rules and the rules of the FDA, you would inform the doctor of the product's contraindication. But let's take that out of the equation for a moment.

There are two forces that every sales professional must deal with. One is meeting your company's expectation for growth in your territory. We all know this as a quota, and the penalty for not reaching it can be the loss of a bonus, a reduction in commission or even termination. Even though most medical companies emphasize the requirement of full disclosure to the healthcare provider, as a salesperson, you may be feeling some pressure to meet the company's sales goals as more important at a given moment. But, *nothing is ever more important than the patient's health and well-being.*

The other pressure is the desire or need to maximize income. Most people enter medical sales to earn a professional level income, and there is nothing wrong with that. We all need to pay our bills, and if you're just starting out, just making ends meet may be a challenge. But, focusing on the sales commission when a patient's life and health could be on the line is nothing more than selfish greed.

Nothing is more important than the patient

Nothing is more important than the patient, even if it means causing some irritation to your customers. Several years ago, I brought a product into the operating room for evaluation during a surgical procedure. As the surgeon was getting ready to make the incision, I noticed a housefly had found his way into the operating room and landed on a sterile drape covering the patient. Whenever anything that is not sterile contacts the sterile field, the field is considered contaminated and the patient is at risk of infection, especially with something as dirty as a fly. No one else in the room saw the fly and I had to tell someone. I motioned for Debbie, the nurse who was scrubbed in on the surgery to come over.

I whispered, "Debbie, a fly just landed on the drape."

Debbie did not look too happy about the prospect of having to tell the surgeon. The surgery would not be able to start until everything that was sterile was replaced or re-sterilized, not to mention feeling the wrath of an unhappy surgeon whose case will be delayed by at least 30 minutes.

Debbie whispered back, "It's okay I don't think the surgeon saw the fly."

I was flabbergasted by her response. The surgeon was performing an orthopedic procedure, where he would be cutting into bone. Infections that occur in bone can be very difficult to treat and can last a lifetime. The worst case scenario included amputation or even death. I did not want to alienate Debbie, because she had a say in many of the buying decisions involving my products at that hospital. But I could not bear the thought of some patient getting a serious infection because I did not speak up.

I whispered, "Debbie, either you tell him or I'm going to tell him."

She gave me a dirty look and then turned around and told the surgeon about the fly. No one was happy about the delay and the ensuing extra work, but the bottom line is that it was the right thing for the patient. I never had any repercussions from Debbie, because she knew telling the surgeon was the right thing to do.

Respecting the patient's privacy is another key component of ethical medical sales. In fact, it is the law. The Health Insurance Portability and Accountability Act (HIPAA) was enacted by the U.S. Congress in 1996. The Privacy Rule, which took effect April 13, 2003, established regulations for the use and disclosure of Protected Health Information (PHI). PHI is any information about health status, provision of health care or payment for health care that can be linked to an individual. This is interpreted rather broadly and includes any part of a patient's medical record or payment history. When health care providers and their associated facilities disclose PHI to facilitate treatment, payment or health care operations, they must make a reasonable effort to disclose only the minimum necessary information required to achieve its purpose. The Privacy Rule requires covered entities to take reasonable steps to ensure the confidentiality of communications with individuals[1]. This includes sharing information with medical sales representatives who are directly or indirectly involved with a patient's care.

Let's step away from the legal implications of privacy and look at it from the ethical perspective. The doctor-patient relationship requires that all health issues, including those of the most personal nature, be disclosed in the interest of medical care. Any time this personal information is disclosed to you as a medical sales professional in the course of doing your job, you have a moral obligation, as well as a legal one, to respect the patient's privacy at all times. This means never discussing or disclosing this private information except with those medical professionals directly involved with that patient's care. You are also ethically and legally required to be sure the privacy cannot be breached by only discussing the patient in a secure location where your conversation cannot be overheard. For example, discussing Mrs. Smith's chest X-ray in the hospital elevator not only violates the HIPAA policy guidelines, it also violates the trust Mrs. Smith places in medical professionals to keep her information confidential.

Ethics also applies when it comes to discussing health care providers. You could find yourself in a situation where one doctor will inquire about another doctor's skills or methods of practice. Don't make the mistake of believing that dishing on a doctor's competitors is a good way to build rapport. It will do the opposite. When a doctor hears you

---

[1] www.hhs.gov/ocrhipaa/

badmouthing another doctor to him, he may be wondering, "If he talks this way about Dr. X., then what does he say about me?" The best way to handle any questions about another doctor's skills, practice or temperament is to defer the question by saying that it would be unprofessional for you to discuss other surgeons. The vast majority of health care providers will respect you for this, and it will go a long way towards building their trust in you.

Personal Integrity

When your customers see you as someone with integrity, they will never question whether or not you will do the right thing. They know that you will.

Some people tend not to trust salespeople, and here is the number one reason why—too many salespeople make all kinds of commitments, and then don't honor them. It's such a simple rule: ***Always do what you say you are going to do.*** Yet, many people in the profession of medical sales violate it. It's not that that they don't have good intentions. I believe the problem is that so many people in this profession don't take the time to consider the implications and real possibilities of delivering on their commitments. Many sales representatives make promises and then forget that they made them. Consequently, the promises go unfulfilled and their integrity is lost.

Honor Your Commitments

When I left medical selling to pursue speaking and training full-time, I visited with most of my customers to thank them for their business and friendship over the years. Many complimented me on how well I performed as a sales professional and I asked them, "Why did you do business with me all these years?" Some of them told me that

I represented good products or had good technical knowledge. But the number one reason my customers told me they did business with me was that *I always did what I said I was going to do*. I would reply in astonishment, "Don't all reps do what they say they are going to do?" The answer was always along the lines of, "No, not always." The ones that do are the ones successfully earning professional level incomes.

When you make a commitment, you must take steps to ensure that you will be able to honor that commitment. I always entered every commitment in my PDA, with an alarm to remind me of the due date, regardless of how trivial the commitment may have seemed. Even if I did not have an answer or solution when I said I would, I would always contact the customer with a simple, "I want you to know I'm still working on it and haven't forgotten," message. I suggest you do the same. It will go a long way toward demonstrating your integrity and commitment to your customers.

Underpromise and Overdeliver

Again, this is what makes medical sales different. If you're selling copy machines and you fail to honor a commitment, your customer will be displeased because he is not getting good copies. When you fail to honor a commitment to a healthcare provider, it interferes with his or her ability to provide optimal care to the patient.

One of the best pieces of advice I received in my sales career is to *"underpromise and overdeliver."* For example, if a customer tells you that she needs to receive your product on May 16th and you find out that it is backordered until May 18th, and an earlier delivery date is possible, here is how you might handle it. First, tell the customer the truth! Tell them that it won't be released until May 18th and with shipping, you probably won't be able to get it into her hands before

May 20th. In reality, you have underpromised, because overnight shipping could get the product to the customer on May 19th. When the product shows up on May 19th, you will have overdelivered, because the customer was not expecting the product to arrive until May 20th. Contrast the customer's feelings to a situation in which you promise the product for May 19th and, due to a glitch, it doesn't arrive until May 20th—you will have an unhappy customer!

Always Tell the Truth

Telling the truth is one of the first things your mother or father taught you, once you were old enough to understand. Unfortunately, there are still legions of salespeople who still have not learned this by adulthood. Always tell the truth, especially when someone's life and well-being are depending on it. There are going to be times when you want to save face with a customer. Perhaps you made a mistake or forgot something, or have been habitually late for your appointments. The way to save face is not to lie about it, but to explain how you will correct the behavior that caused the problem to avoid it happening in the future.

Lying may not catch up to you right away, but sooner or later it will. Jack was one of my biggest competitors. He was very successful, although he developed a reputation over the years that led many not to trust him. Jack was such a skilled liar that even when you knew he was not telling the truth, a part of you still believed him! Jack's customers had diminished over the years due to his various shenanigans, but this one was Jack's *piece de resistance*. It was Jack's responsibility to check the inventory cart at his biggest hospital account before any surgeries. One day, during a surgical procedure, the correct size of Jack's product was missing from the cart. An emergency phone call was placed to Jack to inform him. He vehemently asserted that he had checked the inventory the day before and that he knew the size they were looking for was on the cart. Because the correct size was not found and getting another one from Jack would take hours, an alternative size had to be used. As a result, the patient did not get the best possible result.

Immediately following the surgery, the surgeon personally went through the inventory cart, removing every item, one by one. The missing product was definitely not there. The following morning, Jack arrived at the hospital and approached the surgeon who had performed the previous day's surgery. He said, "Doctor, I just checked the cart, and like I said, the product you are looking for is there."

The doctor responded, "Bull*hit! I checked the cart myself. It wasn't there."

Jack said, "It's there . . . I'll show you," as he walked the surgeon over to the cart, opened it and pointed to the "missing" product. What Jack failed to realize was that a scrub tech saw him walk into the inventory room of the hospital about an hour earlier, carrying product—the missing product. Jack tried to cover his tracks by stealthily placing the missing product into inventory after the fact and then lying to the surgeon's face!

What was the outcome? Jack was instructed to collect all of his inventory and leave the hospital. He was also informed that he was barred from entering the building. Jack's company lost $2 million worth of business in an instant and Jack lost his job, all because he didn't do what he said he was going to do (check the inventory before surgeries), and then lied. Despite many successful years in the business, no one would hire Jack because of his soiled reputation.

There are two things that Jack should have done to protect his integrity. The first is to do what he said he was going to do, which was check the inventory. The second was to have owned up to his mistake publicly and convince the surgeon and hospital that it would never happen again.

We are all human. You *will* make mistakes in your medical sales career. Just be up front and honest about it and proactive in preventing a recurrence. In fact, a mistake is a great opportunity to let the customer know that you will always be honest with them, regardless of how embarrassed you are or the potential consequences that you may face as a result. Look for ways to demonstrate a positive outcome of the situation. For example, Jack could have used the inventory debacle as an opportunity to demonstrate an improvement in how he manages inventory and performs his job as a medical sales professional. Instead, he tried to save his hide by lying. Sure, Jack was punished, but unfortunately, the patient could have paid quite a price for Jack's lack of integrity.

Telling the Truth Means Full Disclosure

There may be instances in your career when you'll be deciding whether or not you need to disclose something to a customer about your product or service, or a situation. If you're ever in doubt as to what to do, it is better to disclose the information to your healthcare customer and allow him or her to decide what is best for the patient. If you're not sure, ask yourself these questions:

- Could withholding this information affect the treatment outcome of a patient?
- Could withholding this information affect the healthcare provider's ability to provide optimum care for the patient?
- Could withholding this information compromise your business relationship with the customer in any way?

• Could I be violating any state or federal laws or company rules that require me to disclose the information to the healthcare provider?

Part of ethics and integrity is making your healthcare provider customers and staffs fully aware of any potential problems prior to the time that they will be using your products or services. For example, if your company has a backorder situation or you are missing inventory, the time to tell the customer is prior to the time that they will be using your product or service—not during or after. I know of too many circumstances where inventories were incomplete or equipment was not operational, and this information was not disclosed in the hope that what was missing or broken would not be needed. This is wrong! Don't ever allow your customers to put their patients in this position without full disclosure.

You Are Responsible For Everything That Happens In Your Business

Things sometimes go wrong in medical sales, and people with integrity don't try to pass the blame when it happens. Will things happen that are beyond your control? Of course, but your customer still expects you to do all that you can to solve the problem. It is very easy to point fingers and try to transfer blame.

"My company didn't ship the right product."

"The office screwed up."

"My assistant/junior sales associate had not been to training yet."

"Overnight delivery sent the package to the wrong location."

"The clinic employee is incompetent."

Your territory is your ship. Because you're the one in charge, assume command. It is your job to make sure that your products and services are available, on time, in good condition and with the proper technical support for your customers and their patients. When things go wrong, let people know that you assume responsibility and fix the problem so it doesn't happen again. Adopt the mantra, "My ship— my responsibility," and people will respect your integrity.

When all is said and done, customers will buy from you if they see you as competent, know you deliver on your promises and can be expected to do the right thing. When customers think of you in those terms, your reputation will carry you well throughout your career.

Several months went by and Brad was feeling more comfortable in his new sales role. He tried on numerous occasions to schedule another appointment with Dr. Clark, but the doctor's secretary told Brad that Dr. Clark was happy with what he was using and "didn't want to waste Brad's time." What changed?

When Healthcare providers consult with you regarding your products and services, they trust that you are the expert on those products and services. They look to you as an authority and resource as to how your products and services can help them to better care for their patients, while avoiding any problems or complications. Your customers must see you as an asset! Brad's blatant admission of his lack of confidence not only killed his opportunity with Dr. Clark, but it also led the doctor to view Brad as a liability.

Healthcare providers assume a huge responsibility caring for patients. Their job is to do everything they can to improve the patient's health and quality of life. The first rule of medicine is, "Do no harm." If any healthcare provider sees you, your company or your products and services as potentially harming a patient, the relationship is over.

Healthcare professionals like salespeople who are competent and confident. Your confidence and belief in your products and what they can do for the patient sell as much, and at times more, than what you say. You sell solutions, and if you don't have absolute confidence in those solutions and your ability to help provide them, no one else will, either. You can't fake true confidence.

How do you develop the kind of confidence you need to succeed in medical selling? I believe that confidence comes from three things:

Knowledge • Preparation • Experience

Knowledge

When you enter medical sales, you have become a student for the rest of your career. Knowledge in medicine is endless, and as current technology evolves and new technology is introduced, the base of knowledge that is available grows exponentially. This means that part of your professional life is continually educating yourself about everything that affects what you sell. This requires continuous effort and dedication. The life of a medical sales representative is busy, to say the least. You need to schedule "learning time" in the evenings, during lunch and on weekends.

Always carry articles and study materials with you to read during downtime between appointments and when waiting to see healthcare providers in their offices. Find out if your company provides audio programs on CD or mp3 that you can listen to as you drive between sales calls. If they don't, suggest it. Learning takes commitment and effort, but it's not optional. If your competitor knows more than you, then there is a chance he will sell more than you. Don't let that happen. No matter how you do it, or when you do it, just *do it!*

Preparation

Preparation is what you do to get ready for a sales presentation or to service a customer. Salespeople who fail to adequately prepare are never as fully confident as those who do. A lack of preparation causes confidence to erode into hope. "Gosh, I hope the doctor doesn't ask me how that works." "I hope they figure a way to treat the patient without using my product." "I hope this thing works as it's supposed to." "I hope that the courier shows up on time." Barack Obama[2] said that "Hope is not a plan." Yet I have seen too many sales professionals operate more on hope than preparation. You have too much on the line

---

[2] The Audacity of Hope, Barack Obama, 2006

as a medical sales professional to not be properly prepared.

Many medical sales representatives describe their job as being stressful. There is no question that medical sales can and often does place the representative in stressful situations. But too often, the resulting stress is a product of poor preparation. Take time to prepare and you will sleep better at night and approach each day and each situation with confidence.

Experience

When it comes to confidence, nothing can take the place of experience. The longer you work in any segment of the medical device and equipment industry, the more knowledgeable you will be about navigating the environment, the needs of the players and how to deal with unexpected events that come in your way.

If you are just beginning your medical sales career, take comfort in knowing that your confidence will grow as you spend time learning, preparing and just "doing it." In the interim, don't skimp on education in sales and product knowledge. Do all you can to build your confidence and to project that confidence to your customers.

If you are shifting sales positions to a different segment or medical specialty, recognize that your confidence may suffer, just as Brad's did in the previous story. Just take it one day at a time, one product at a time and one customer at a time. Learn one product well enough to make a sales presentation, handle basic questions and get an evaluation. Always be honest with your customers regarding your experience with any product, but don't freak them out ahead of time, like Brad did, by telling them how little you know.

Beware of false confidence

Many medical sales reps adopt a "fake it 'til you make it" attitude when it comes to confidence. False confidence is no substitute for knowledge, preparation and experience, and the healthcare experts you're dealing with will quickly see through it.

Don't make the mistake of letting *false confidence* lull you into thinking you have what you need to do the job. When I first got my pilot's license and had a whopping 70 hours in my log book, like most new pilots, I couldn't wait to take people for airplane rides—and I did! One day, I took Earl, a friend of mine, for a ride. Just after take-off, I was supposed to level off at 2,000 feet to avoid entering controlled airspace without a clearance, but I was way too busy enjoying Earl's wonderment upon leaving the ground. Suddenly, I got a radio call from the tower telling me to contact air traffic control about the airspace I had just intruded into. That controller read me the riot act, including threatening me with a violation (the equivalent of a traffic ticket, only worse!). I looked over at my friend Earl, who was giving me a "Do you know what you're doing?" look.

I mumbled something like, "That airspace was so close to the airport. Those things happen—nothing to worry about." I did my best to put on the "confident pilot" act. Earl nodded and we had a nice flight.

After we landed, I asked Earl how he enjoyed the flight. He said,"Mace, it was great. But when that controller was chastising you, you looked like your confidence went out the window, and I was a little concerned. I was a bit nervous because when I looked over at you, it seemed like you were trying to cover up your lost confidence." I was.

Two-thousand-four-hundred hours later, it frightens me to think about all the people I took flying in my early days of piloting, because I realize now what I didn't know then. I also know what I don't know

now, which helps me to make good piloting decisions and prevents bad situations. Thanks to experience, I have a lot of confidence in my piloting abilities and don't need to fake it for my passengers, like I did during my first few hundred hours. I may have pulled the wool over a few people's eyes in my early flying days, but I often wonder how many of my passengers saw right through my false-confidence, just as Earl did.

Authentic Confidence

Confidence in medical sales is essential. It affects everything you do—how you prospect, how you present, how you follow-up, how you handle rejection—everything. Confidence is even a useful tool for getting into places you need to go, such as doctor's offices and hospitals.

I would frequently get called to the operating room at all hours of the day and night. Hospital security wasn't as strict as it has been since 9/11, but it existed. There would be a surgical team waiting for me to bring a product or guide them through a procedure, and to save time, I would sometimes rush past security, which by the way, is something I advise you *never* to do (security is a serious issue since 9/11 and failure to obey the rules can get your barred from a hospital—*or even arrested!*).

I would always look the security guard squarely in the eye and say, "Good evening" or "Good afternoon," as I passed, just as many of the hospital staff did.

In more than 20 years of doing this, do you know how many times I was stopped and had someone ask me, "Who are you and what is your business?" Only once, and when I explained who I was, he let me walk through. People will seldom try to stop someone who is confidently moving with purpose. Again, I do not advise you to play this game today—*in fact, you should make it a point to always go through security and abide by all hospital and clinic security rules, or you probably won't be allowed to return.* I'm just offering it as an example of the power of confidence, even if I once misused it (and now seek absolution by confessing my sins!).

How to Look Confident (even if you're not)

If you're lacking confidence as you perform your medical sales job, it's a sign that you aren't prepared and might be getting in over your head. Never lie about what you know or don't know—it could compromise a patient's well-being and destroy your relationship with the customer. But at least always try to look confident, even when you're not. The best way to do this is to:

- Speak slowly and deliberately—speaking in a calm and relaxed manner helps convey confidence.
- Breathe at a relaxed pace—it will help keep you calm. You won't look very confident if you're holding your breath (and turning blue) or hyperventilating—be aware of your breathing.
- Smile—people who lack confidence don't smile. Smiling will help you relax and feel more self-assured. Of course, don't smile if everything is heading downhill.

Real confidence evolves over time—there are no shortcuts. Become competent and you'll feel confident. Your customers will sense that they are doing business with the right company, the right product or service and the right medical sales professional. Don't scare them out of doing business with you like Brad, the disclaimer sales guy, did. Do all you can to honor their expectations and you will be richly rewarded throughout your career.

8

The Medical Sales Attitude

It's 5 P.M. on a Friday afternoon. You've put in a week of hard work and you're ready to head to the local pub to meet some friends for happy hour to unwind. Your cell phone rings, and it's a doctor who has an emergency need for one of your products. He asks if you can meet him at the hospital at 6 p.m. with the required equipment, so he can treat a patient. You tell the doctor you'll be there and then you call your friends to tell them you can't make the happy hour.

There is a possibility that your attitude has changed from what you were feeling as you were heading toward the Friday celebration with your friends. You're no longer going to party—you're going to work! What is your attitude?

Ideally, your attitude is one of opportunity and optimism. A customer called you, instead of one of your competitors, and you now have the opportunity to spend time with him and support his decision to use your products by providing expertise and good service. Plus, you will also be earning a nice commission, which not only eases the pain of not being able to hoist a drink or two with your friends, but it actually thrills the heck out of you. You like making money!

You drive the 30 minutes to your local office or warehouse to pick up the equipment that you need, and then meet the doctor at the appointed time at the hospital. When he sees you, he says, "Thanks so much for coming in on such short notice on a Friday evening. I'm sure you had other plans, but my patient in the emergency room needs this done right away, and the new product you showed me seems like it is ideal for what I need to do. I hope you had something to eat, because we are going to be in for a long night."

If you're excited and happy to be there and genuinely grateful for the opportunity, then you will probably reply, "Doctor—no problem—thank you so much for calling me. I have everything you need, and I will be here with you for as long as you need me. I appreciate the opportunity."

Flexibility is part of the game

Doctors like sales representatives who are flexible and will show up on short notice and have a "can-do" attitude. Chances are he's not happy to be working on a Friday night either, but if he must, it's better to work with people on his team who have a positive attitude and are willing to do whatever it takes to get the job done.

Next, you head to the operating room to instruct the O.R. team on how to set up and use your equipment. When you get there, several of the O.R. staff are not happy to be there on a Friday night. One of the nurses tells you about the concert she is going to miss and the money she just wasted on the tickets. The nurse anesthetist keeps saying, "I don't know why this couldn't wait until morning!" On the other hand, the O.R. tech who will be scrubbing in with the doctor says that he looks forward to being called in and earning time-and-a-half pay when he's on call because he's saving up to buy a new motorcycle. At least somebody has a positive attitude about working. You can commiserate with the unhappy nurse and tell her all about your evening plans that got fouled, or you can share the sentiments of the surgical technician and take pleasure in the fact that you are working toward one of your goals—building your business! You get to decide.

Realistically, no one expects you to be genuinely joyful about needing to change plans with friends and work unexpectedly. It just comes with the territory. Having an attitude that shows you understand this is appreciated by your customers and is good for your long-term business.

Attitude is a compelling driver in terms of the companies and the sales reps customers choose to do business with. Doctors and other health care providers have little patience for bad attitudes in medical sales people, because every day, as health care providers, they need to perform tasks that they may not feel like doing, but patient care demands it. They know you are paid when they call you and if you don't want the business, someone else does. Your customers *expect* you to have a positive attitude.

Notice I did not say that you need to "act" like you have a positive attitude—that will only get you so far. Attitude comes from within. Your real attitude is often palpable, despite your best efforts to conceal it. Find a positive way to view the circumstances, even if it's as simple as you're getting paid instead of a competitor. *If you are not capable of changing your attitude, then do what you must to avoid showing your distain for the customer or situation.* But at some level, some of your customers will sense your sentiment, even if it isn't blatantly obvious.

Human beings have the ability to control their attitudes in the face of almost any situation. Viktor Frankl[3] said, "Everything can be taken from a man but . . . the last of the human freedoms—to choose one's attitude in any given set of circumstances, to choose one's own way."

---

[3] Man's Search For Meaning, Frankl, Victor. 1946, p. 104

Frankl showed that even under the worst possible circumstances—being mentally and physically tortured in a Nazi concentration camp for years, you still get to choose your attitude.

Gratitude

A good attitude starts with gratitude. This isn't cliché motivational speaker mumbo-jumbo . . . it's true. Whenever you are faced with an unpleasant task in your job (or anywhere else in your life, for that matter) you need to find things to be thankful about in that situation. Let's go back to the situation where you get called into work with a customer and are disappointed with having to suddenly change your plans. How can you create and maintain a positive mental attitude?

According to my friend and fellow speaker, Dr. Larry Duboff (LarryDuboff.com), you should make a gratitude list. Write out all the things you are grateful for in any situation. Your gratitude list for the scenario I've been discussing might look like this:

Things I am grateful for about having to cancel plans with my friends and work with Dr. Jones until 3 A.M.:

- I get to help a patient.
- I get to spend time with Dr. Jones, who is normally very difficult to see.
- Dr. Jones called me for his surgery—he could have called my competitor.
- I get to score points with Dr. Jones by being available whenever he needs me and working into the night with a good attitude.
- This could lead to ongoing business with Dr. Jones.
- It's an opportunity to develop a closer relationship with the employees in the hospital.
- I get to learn.
- I get paid.

Does it make more sense to focus on the things you're grateful for, instead of the beer and sleep that you're missing? If you're not saying, "Heck, yeah!" I hope you're re-evaluating your career choice.

Three winning attitudes

Here are three attitudes that play well with customers. Once these become ingrained in you, your customers will consistently perceive your attitude in a positive light:

1. **Gratitude**—Thank-you for the opportunity to work with you and provide you with products and services for the patients that you serve.
2. **Service**—My purpose is to provide you with the products and services that you need to provide care to your patients. I'm going to do all that I can to fulfill your expectations. Even if I can't guarantee the results, I will always do the very best that I can.
3. **Confidence**—I am competent in the knowledge and skills necessary to help you use my product or service.

Health care providers prefer working with medical sales professionals who show up with *consistently positive, upbeat attitudes*. Don't sabotage all of your selling efforts by ignoring this important reality.

The Key Attitude in Any Selling Situation: Expect the Sale

When you have a sales conversation with a prospect or customer, do you expect to make the sale? *Every time?*

"Expecting the sale" is a critical attitude for medical sales professionals. It shows that you have absolute belief in what you're offering your customers and that you believe it is the best choice for their patients. It allows your confidence to come through without hesitation.

Here's the key to expecting to make the sale—you must believe it yourself! If you don't think that you truly have a shot in getting your prospect or customer to say "Yes" to what you're offering, then why are you selling it?

Anytime you're in a sales situation, speak as if the customer will be doing business with you. There is an absolute magic to this! Convince yourself before and during every sales conversation that the customer is going to buy. Even if you don't always make the sale, you'll make more sales when you expect it than when you don't.

Medical Sales Attitude Rules

- If your attitude is "leaning the wrong way," make sure you fix it before you spend time with customers.
- You CAN control your attitude in any situation—there are no excuses!
- Never let a bad attitude show. If you can't shake it, keep it to yourself and display a pleasant demeanor to the customer.
- Expect the sale (without being cocky or arrogant).
- Always display a "can-do," or at the least a "will-try," attitude.
- Use gratitude and acceptance to control your attitude in situations where you have no control.
- Maintain a consistent, positive attitude with everyone you meet, including your family, friends and co-workers.
- Never make excuses for a bad attitude—your customers are not interested.

9

The Essential Medical Sales Skills

You must have the right skills to succeed in medical sales, but what are the right skills?

Certainly, selling skills are at the top of the list, but there are two additional skill sets a medical sales rep must have: technical skills and relationship skills. Even sales managers, distributors and human resource managers don't always agree upon which is most important for medical sales professionals.

From an outsider's perspective, it would seem that technical skills are more important, because medical devices can be extremely complex and you must be able to converse at the same technical level as the healthcare customer with respect to your product or service. But technical skills alone won't cut it.

People are sometimes hired for sales from clinical positions because they possess technical skills for certain products or services. Tom, a pacemaker representative I knew for many years, needed a junior sales associate to provide technical assistance to surgeons in the operating room while they were implanting his company's pacemakers. Debbie, who worked at one of Tom's hospital accounts, seemed like a good candidate. She had scrubbed in on cardiovascular cases for years and knew Tom's pacemaker line almost as well as Tom, so he hired her.

Debbie did fine when she covered surgeries for Tom in the hospital where she used to work, but things did not go well for Debbie in Tom's other hospital accounts. Why not? The people in the other accounts did not like Debbie. They found her to be condescending and arrogant, to the point of trying to tell experienced vascular surgeons how they should be performing surgery (a big no-no)! Tom did what he could for damage control, but the overall sentiment from Tom's customers was to keep Debbie away from them if he wished to enjoy their continued business.

Debbie knew her stuff—no one could have walked into her job with better technical skills. She knew how to cross-reference the right pacemaker leads, program the pacemakers and troubleshoot almost any problem. But that wasn't enough. She just didn't have the necessary relationship skills. Tom tried to teach her these skills, but eventually had to terminate her employment.

There are many jobs in the world where technical skills are all that you need to succeed—take engineering, accounting or working on an assembly line, for example. Even a doctor who is known for great diagnostic and surgical skills can get by with a poor bedside manner if his superior medical skills are known throughout the community. In the sales world however, relationship skills are not an option—they are a requirement.

Many studies have been done over the years where starting salespeople were assessed and scored to determine whether they had stronger relationship skills or technical sales skills. Reviewing the achievement levels of these salespeople 10, 20 and even 30 years later consistently showed that salespeople with strong relationship skills were vastly more successful than those who had strong technical skills.

Don't get me wrong—medical sales requires solid technical skills in order to understand what you need to know and effectively communicate the information to your customers. But you must also establish rapport in which people like you and trust you, if you expect them to buy from you.

Use Relationship Skills

Relationship skills are "people skills." If you don't like people or have difficulty getting along with them, your medical sales career will be a struggle (as will other areas of your life).

Medical sales professionals must continuously establish, nurture and maintain business relationships. Some salespeople don't understand that medical sales means you're playing for the long term, not just the sale at the moment. Don't ever make the mistake of looking at a customer as just a transaction—this is what short-sighted, struggling sales people do. Each customer is an *asset* that must be managed long-term.

Can you strengthen your relationship skills? Absolutely! Let's start with an inventory of where you stand currently. I consider the following relationship skills to be essential for all medical sales professionals.

Practice Verbal Skills

This is the ability to speak well by clearly expressing your thoughts, so that the meaning is unambiguous. It is not only what you say, but also *how you say it*. You will learn that medical professionals do not like being corrected (as Debbie discovered) by salespeople, unless it is done respectfully and appropriately. You must speak to your medical customers in ways that they do not find to be insulting or demeaning.

Develop Judgment Skills

Judgment is difficult to teach, and is usually learned through experience. When you show good judgment, it strengthens your business relationships because your customers will trust your advice. Always consider the ramifications of everything that you do. In other words, think things out before you act. Try to use the best common sense that you have, and when in doubt, seek counsel from someone you respect who understands your business.

Build Trust

As the famous speaker Bill Gove said, "Once people trust you, then you can fly." Trust is probably the number one relationship factor in life, and it indeed crosses into medical sales. Healthcare providers must trust you enough to believe that you would never do anything to compromise their reputations or their patients' health and safety. Always speak the truth about your products and services and always do what you say you are going to do. Often, if trust is lost, there are no second chances.

Be Likeable

This is one of the most powerful relationship skills, for the obvious reason that few people want to spend time with someone they don't like. What makes a medical sales professional likeable? Here's the short list: they are happy, smile frequently, treat all people well, don't complain, have a can-do attitude, are friendly and people generally feel good being around them.

Meet Expectations

Customers have expectations of you, both stated and unstated, in business dealings. Expectations should always be clearly defined by discussing them with your customers in detail. There may even be times when you should put those expectations in writing to avoid misunderstandings. You must always honor your customers' expectations, unless you discuss changes in advance.

Meeting expectations can be simply defined this way: do what your customer is expecting you to do! It sounds simple, but I have taken more business from competitors over their failure to do this one simple thing than anything else. Your healthcare customers depend on you to deliver goods and services as expected, so they can focus on patient care. Do your best not to disappoint them—they may not forgive you if you do.

Address and Correct Problems

It is a given that problems will arise from time to time as customers are using your product or services. Part of your job is to handle these situations in a timely manner and keep your customers informed of the progress. Never withhold information that could affect a patient's outcome.

Be Consistent

This is another biggie. Customers don't want to feel that they can count on you now and then. They need to know that you will come through for them each and every time. "Most of the time" doesn't cut it when patients' lives are on the line.

Relate to the Customer on Their Level

This means that you understand how everything you do or say affects the customer in his or her professional practice and life. See things through their eyes and respond accordingly. When they think of you, you want them to always feel, "He understands my world!"

Be Outgoing

Customers expect salespeople to be outgoing; not overwhelming, but in a way that shows you are willing to make the effort to connect with people. Shyness is often viewed as antisocial. If you suffer from shyness, you must either get over it or make a conscious effort to push past it.

Be a Good Listener

This is one of the key selling skills, and certainly one of the key relationship skills. Your customers are not interested in your solutions until they are sure that you understand their problems and challenges. The only way this can happen is if you listen more than you talk. I will cover this later in the section on sales presentation skills. Remember, hearing is only the ability to detect sounds with your ears. *Listening* is when you *hear and understand* what people are saying.

Be Empathic

Healthcare professionals experience many emotions as a result of their jobs. When you show them that you understand what they are feeling, as opposed to just telling them, you can create a bond that's hard to break. For example, if you know your customer has had a bad day because of a critical event and you have a sales presentation planned, you may not want to just tell them that you understand, and then move forward with the presentation. Instead, ask if there is anything that you can do. Offer to postpone the presentation until a more appropriate time. Don't make *them* ask *you*!

Resolve Conflicts

Conflict can be a part of any relationship, whether it's a marriage, a friendship or a business relationship. Should a conflict arise with a customer, address it and do what you can to resolve it. Some medical sales professionals let things cool down before contacting an angry customer and at times, that's a good idea. Make sure you don't ignore the customer's concerns or feelings. Pretending that a bad event didn't happen won't make it go away—it will usually just make the situation worse. Take customer concerns seriously. Whether the customer is right or not, remember that perception is reality—whatever a customer is feeling is real to them. Address all conflicts in a timely manner, regardless of who is at fault. It's the right thing to do and your customers expect it.

Treat Everyone You Meet In The Course of Business As If That Person Is Important To Your Business

Mary Kay Ash, the founder of Mary Kay Cosmetics, used to teach her consultants to imagine that everyone they meet is wearing a sign around their neck that says, "Make Me Feel Important."

A common mistake made by too many medical sales professionals is failing to treat every person they meet in their accounts as if that person is important to their business. It's easy to pay attention to those people who influence the sale of your products, such as a staff member who can issue a purchase order or give final approval to a purchase. Early in my selling days, someone gave me some advice that yielded big dividends throughout my career: "Learn the name of every person that you encounter, everywhere you do business, and greet them by name."

I'm talking about learning *the name of every person* you meet at your hospitals, clinics and doctors' offices. This includes security guards, housekeeping and maintenance personnel, orderlies, unit secretaries, receptionists, hospital administrators and their staffs, cafeteria employees, car valets—I mean *everyone*! Here is why it is worth the effort to learn everyone's name:

- Your competition probably does not do this—they only establish relationships with people who can help them to complete a sale or do their jobs. You look good when you do things that other sales reps refuse to do, that your customers appreciate. Or, if your competition does know and use everyone's name, you need to do it, too!

- People notice how you treat and relate to other people. When you are friendly to everyone in your accounts, your friendliness appears genuine, and not motivated by personal gain.

- When people like you, they tell others. Everything that a customer hears about you from anyone, negative or positive, will affect his or her thoughts about you at either a conscious or subconscious level. One hospital bought a very expensive piece of capital equipment from me. When the O.R. purchasing agent called to give me the purchase order, she asked if I knew why they were buying it from me. I guessed and said, "I had the best price?" She told me that wasn't it. One of the orderlies overheard the conversation about which vendor to choose and said, "Buy it from Mace. He's the only sales rep who comes here that treats everyone the same. I like him." Because almost everything else was equal with respect to the product, the O.R. purchasing agent told me that the orderly's comment swayed her decision.

- Every person's name is music to his or her ears. When you learn and use everyone's name on a regular basis, it makes them feel good about you as a person. That never hurts in sales.

- Get to know everyone at your company as well, including all of the support personnel. Learn their names and let them know you care about them as people. They are your "inside customers" who also play an important role in your overall success.

Technical Skills

Technical skills are essential for survival in medical sales. Sales people try to fake many things, but it is very difficult to fake technical competency.

New medical sales professionals often confuse the requirement of competency with mastery. Selling to doctors and other healthcare professionals can be intimidating—they are some of the most highly educated and trained people in the workforce. The intimidation factor arises from the belief that you need to know as much as they do. You certainly need to have a competent working knowledge of your products, but unless you go to medical school or have worked as a healthcare provider, you can't have the depth of expertise that they have. Here's the good part—you don't need to!

Medical professionals are *experts* in their field. Let them be the experts! Don't try to show how much you know, or think you will dazzle them with your knowledge. They like being the experts and are seldom impressed by a sales rep who's trying to "teach them" things they have mastered. However, they do expect you to be *competent* in terms of knowing your products or services and your ability to guide them in their appropriate use.

Competency is the result of focused learning. Most all companies provide their sales reps with the technical information and training necessary to effectively sell their products or services. True competency requires that you go beyond solely what the company provides. Information is available everywhere today—in the library and online in professional journals. Your customers can be one of your best sources of learning, because they are the experts and many of them love to teach. Believe it or not, most will be more impressed by you if you ask them to teach you what you don't know than when you try to show them how much you do.

Here are some ways to acquire technical competency:

- Study company-generated product information completely, including package insert information. Seek clarification of anything that you do not understand.
- Study technical protocols or guidebooks created for the medical professional utilizing the product or service.
- Review videos that have been produced about how to properly use the product or service.
- Review all product information on your company's website.
- Get someone who knows the product to conduct a "hands-on" workshop with you on the product or service. This could be a product manager from the company or a more experienced salesperson.
- Obtain a sample of the product or the equipment that is used in performing your service and spend time familiarizing yourself with it until you feel completely comfortable.
- Ask your customers if you can observe them using your product or service. If you have not yet developed a relationship in which you feel you can do this, then ask a fellow sales associate if one of his or her customers will allow you to observe your product being used.
- Ask your customers to teach you the intricacies of using your product or service (i.e., tips and tricks they use that you can share with other customers).
- Make sure that you learn the necessary technical language (medical

terminology) and feel comfortable using the terms correctly with the proper pronunciation. Mispronouncing medical terms can make you look like a rookie.

Technical competency does not mean that you have all of the information in your head. Competency includes compiling and organizing pertinent reference materials that you will have access to at all times, especially when your customers are using your products or services to treat patients. This includes product profilers, templates, measuring tools, data and tables,stored on your laptop or PDA, and knowing who to contact at your company to answer the questions that you cannot.

Become the Triple Threat

I've discussed two of the essential success skills for medical sales professionals in this chapter. There is one more critical skill that I will spend much time discussing in the rest of the book: selling skills.

When you are competent in what I consider to be the three main skills of medical sales—relationship skills, technical skills, and selling skills—you become a triple threat. Strong competency in any one of these areas can help to offset any weaknesses in the other two, but when you can practice all three and do it well, you pose a real threat to the competition in your territory. Believe it or not, most medical salespeople do not excel at all three skills. Thus if you make the effort to become the *triple threat*, you will know how to take business from your competition and hold onto it.

The only thing that can stop you from being great is you. If you are willing to pay the price of success in this business, (i.e., putting in the time and effort), you will be unstoppable. You will also have an income to match, and that's a wonderful thing. Remember, if medical sales were easy, almost everyone would be doing it. You've already made the choice. You know what it takes. I promise you that it will be worth it.

10

The Key to Successful Medical Sales Presentations: Understand How the Healthcare Provider Thinks

Healthcare providers don't like salespeople. What? You're probably thinking, "My customers love me." That may be true, but if you try to sell them a product that they're really not interested in, they will find you annoying.

What is your primary goal during a sales presentation with a healthcare provider? If it is to sell your product or service, then you are off to a bad start. That makes the sales presentation all about you, instead of all about them. This causes them to look at you as someone who is out to satisfy your own best interests, not theirs. And you expect them to buy from you?

The Healthcare Customer and Change

As a medical sales professional, you offer healthcare providers products or services to improve the quality of care and offer better patient outcomes. You operate from an "excitement of gain" perspective, because you know the great things that your product or service can do. The anticipation of helping healthcare providers and their patients benefit from your company's products compels you to face the challenges of selling in the medical environment. You also want to get paid.

What is a healthcare sales prospect experiencing when a salesperson shows up to sell him or her something? Is it the excitement of gain?

Salespeople are selling *change*. That is the initial perception for most healthcare providers. Answer this important question—how do medical professionals feel about change when it comes to caring for their patients? For most, changing what they are doing is difficult to justify if their patients are getting good results. More importantly, change adds an element of *risk* that most would rather avoid.

Why do healthcare providers often associate change with risk? Unless a clinician is actually seeking better results with a product or service due to a feeling that what they are currently using is inadequate, change introduces a new variable—the possibility of a diminished result, or even harm to the patient. Sometimes, switching products is an easy process, but at times it can involve a complex learning curve. For example, consider a surgeon who needs to change a surgical procedure because of a new product he just switched to. It may take several procedures until the surgeon reaches the same level of comfort and competency that he had before switching. During the time of learning, there is a risk that patients may not get the same good results as the patients before the surgeon switched products.

Let's take it one step further. What happens if a patient receiving the new product has a poor result or is harmed in some way? The patient may sue the doctor for malpractice. That would cost the doctor money and the aggravation of defending or settling the lawsuit. A complaint could also be filed with the state medical board that could put the doctor's license in jeopardy. Bad publicity could damage the doctor's reputation, which might negatively impact his practice in the future. Change offers the possibility that things could improve, but also the chance that things will go wrong. And you thought that all you were asking the prospect to do was to take a look at your product!

The perceived risk of a negative outcome is often responsible for a healthcare provider's lack of enthusiasm when you suggest change. Due to the litigious nature of our society, minimizing risk is a primary consideration, sometimes even more important than what's best for the patient. It's called practicing defensive medicine.

So, as a medical sales professional, you have a choice. You can either approach your prospects and customers in a way that elicits their normal response to risk through change, or you can approach them in a way that will cause them to consider the products and services you sell in a better light.

I used to assume that if I could convince a doctor of a better way of doing something, I would get his business. It worked some of the time, but I learned that many healthcare providers viewed changing products just like one of my customers, Dr. Timmons, did. When I first called on Dr. Timmons to offer him a "better way" of performing a certain surgical procedure, he responded that his current surgical procedure was good. It worked just fine. Of course, because I was there as a salesperson, I thought I asked the right question when I said, "Dr. Timmons, what if I can show you a better way of doing the procedure?"

Dr. Timmons responded with words I will never forget. He said, "Mace, the enemy of good is 'better.'"

I could not contain myself. With a look of disbelief, I said, "What?"

Dr. Timmons explained to me that he has been doing the procedure using his current product for more than 10 years. About five years earlier, he had tried a new product in the hopes of getting a better result. The patient did not do as well and needed to have a second operation to correct the problems the surgeon felt were related to the new product he tried. Dr. Timmons acknowledged that some surgeons were getting better results with the new product, but in his quest for *better*, he took a step backward from the *good* results he had always enjoyed. His thinking made sense.

As I was dejectedly packing up my samples, I asked Dr. Timmons one more question. "Dr. Timmons, are you saying that you will never again try something different from what you are using now?" He said, "Not unless I think there is *a problem* with what I am doing now."

Doesn't it make sense? If you're delivering healthcare and what you're doing is working, and the risk of trying something else might in some way diminish your good results, then why would you want to change? Will you change just because a salesperson is offering you something different or new? Probably not. You may have a few customers that will try something just because it is the newest and they want to be one of the first, but in healthcare, most providers take a more conservative approach.

I realized something that sales trainers have been teaching as long as there have been sales trainers: no problem—no pain—no sale!

It became very clear to me one day that if I could not get my customers to acknowledge some level of "pain" that I could resolve, I was wasting my time. Talking about solutions before identifying or confirming a problem is just ineffective selling.

It's a fact—most salespeople are solutions walking around looking for a problem. They detail their product or service to anyone who will listen, in the hope that the prospect will see some benefit and bite. That's no way to sell, and if this is how you're selling, it's time to stop. A shotgun approach to medical sales will generate some commission dollars, but it's a weak and inefficient method. It forces you to work harder than necessary and it does little, if anything to distinguish yourself and your products from your competitors and their products.

The Automatic Response

I have found that most healthcare professionals have an automatic response when it comes to changing the way they are currently treating patients. This response is preloaded, and they are just waiting for you to give them enough information to deliver it. Their automatic response to whatever you're selling is "*No*."

It's important to understand this pre-programming when you are going into a sales presentation. Medical salespeople and healthcare buyers operate from different perspectives. Hopefully, you are excited about the solutions that your company's products or services deliver to the healthcare professional and the patient. Because you are operating from an excitement of gain perspective, you may assume that you can impart this to your buyer fairly easily. Certainly, the excitement can be transferred with good sales technique, but initially, most buyers in the healthcare profession are concerned about any potential risks to their patients and their reputations when they consider something new. This fear of loss perspective is a direct opposite to the salesperson's operational mindset. Most buyers are spring-loaded to say "No" as soon as you give them a reason.

It's All About Them

Here's something that is probably no surprise to you—doctors and other healthcare professionals tend to have big egos. I don't mean that in a negative way. If they don't have absolute belief that they have the talent and skills to improve a patient's situation, they have no business practicing medicine or treating patients. That requires a healthy ego.

But that ego often carries over into many of the other things that healthcare providers do. Ego can make them believe that they know more than you do about some things when they don't. For the most part, unless your product or service is so drastically different that they have never seen anything like it, they may not be interested in it, at least initially. If all you are talking about up front is your product, your service or your company, they just don't care. In fact, you're probably boring them unless you're talking about their favorite subject—*themselves*! You see, when you call on medical professionals, your presentation needs to be about *them*; not about you, your product or your company. Let me repeat: *the sales conversation needs to be about them!*

Sell to the Little Voice in Your Customer's Head

I'm not suggesting that your customers are psychotic when I talk about the voices in their heads. You have a voice in your head and so do I. I often refer to it as "the little voice."

We all tend to think in words in our mind, as if there were a voice talking to us. For example, as you're reading this, you might be thinking, "Where is he going with this?" or "I think I have heard this stuff before." That's the little voice that I'm talking about. When you are giving a sales presentation to a customer, his or her little voice is responding to everything that you say. In a sense, when you sell to a customer, you are really selling to that little voice.

Wouldn't it be great if you knew what the little voice is saying? That way, instead of just talking to the little voice, you could have a conversation with it! Unless you're a mind reader, there is no way of knowing for sure, but based on experience, you might be able to anticipate or predict what the prospect might be thinking. For example, if you are going over a new surgical procedure that is more complex than the procedure most commonly performed, you might anticipate your prospect's little voice saying, "Wow, this is a lot more involved than what I'm doing now!"

In anticipation of his little voice response, you might say in your presentation, "If this seems a bit more complex than what you are doing now, I'll demonstrate in a moment why it really isn't and how it benefits you and the patient."

When you sell to the little voice, you are keeping the prospect involved in the presentation, instead of letting his little voice run away with his thoughts. Making a statement to the little voice as I suggested is also a good test to determine if the prospect is actually thinking the way you anticipated. For example, if you're testing to see if he thinks the procedure is complex and he does not think that it is, he may respond, "Actually it doesn't seem that complex to me. Please continue."

The customer's facial expression or body language might also be a tip-off that the little voice is in disagreement with or questioning what you are saying. Whenever you sense this, it is wise to stop your presentation and ask, "You look like you have a question or concern about something. May I ask what it is?" Again, this keeps the prospect involved, instead of allowing his little voice to steal his attention away from you.

WIIFM/WIIFMP

Most salespeople know what WIIFM means. As the saying goes, everyone's favorite radio station is WIIFM—"What's In It For Me?" From the moment your prospects or customers notice that you are talking about one of your products or services, consciously or subconsciously they are asking, "What's in it for me?" Healthcare professionals will also be asking WIIFMP, or "What's In It For My Patient?" I wish more sales people would address it in their presentations.

Your entire sales presentation must address the WIIFM question from beginning to end, or you will lose your prospect's attention in a hurry. As mentioned previously, medical professionals are very busy people, with much on their plates. It is easy for their thoughts to take off in directions other than where you want them to go. When you talk about what's in it for them, it holds their attention and delays their automatic response to say no. Therefore, you need to know the WIIFM for your prospect up front and get to it as soon as possible. A strong and compelling WIIFM gets the prospect to focus on potential benefits, instead of potential risks.

When I work with salespeople, either in the field or in a simulated sales situation, most of them begin a presentation by talking about themselves, their company or their product. This does not address WIIFM! Instead, begin your presentation by talking about the prospect and the patient. This moves you closer to their WIIFM.

The next goal in addressing WIIFM is uncovering a problem or level of pain. Your products and services are solutions to problems. It makes no sense to offer a solution until you have identified and discussed a problem you can solve. If there is no problem, there is no WIIFM, yet too many salespeople talk about solutions before finding something to fix. Don't assume that your prospect understands the problem or even acknowledges that a problem exists.

Even if your prospect is familiar with the problems your product or service is designed to solve, unless they can feel "pain" at some level, they won't be very open to your solution. Let me give you a non-medical example that I experienced firsthand.

I have lived in Florida for most of my life. For as far back as I can remember, I would get telemarketing calls a month or two before hurricane season, offering hurricane shutters for my home. The call would go something like this: "We are going to have a sales representative in your area next week who can give you a quote on hurricane shutters for your house and we're offering 40 percent off, this week only." Just like most of you, I too, am spring-loaded to say "No" to telemarketers, especially when I don't see any need for what they are selling. I had never experienced a hurricane in my life, so I had no pain and said "No" quickly to every shutter company that called.

Then, things changed. In 2004 and 2005 my house was damaged by three hurricanes: Frances, Jeanne and Wilma! It looked like South Florida had moved into Mother Nature's target zone for natural disasters. Suddenly, everyone was scrambling for hurricane shutters. The telemarketers weren't calling. Instead, homeowners were calling the shutter companies, and it often took several days to get a call back. A month would pass before a salesperson would come to your house and give you a quote. If you ordered hurricane shutters, the wait was three months to a year to get them manufactured and installed.

What changed in the hurricane shutter business in South Florida? *The pain!* People were worried about their homes and wanted a solution to protect them.

Help Your Healthcare Customers Find the Pain

"Pain" in healthcare comes in many forms. The most obvious is when there is no treatment for a disease or condition. If your product or service offers a new solution to a condition or disease, or an improvement over an existing treatment that still has limitations, you can fix the pain.

Pain also comes in other forms in the health care arena. For example, facilities and healthcare providers can be outpaced by competitors employing newer technology. Several years ago, some progressive orthopedic surgeons started performing joint replacement procedures by making smaller incisions. This was made possible by new surgical instruments that required a different surgical approach. A few surgeons adopted the new technology right away, but many resisted because of the associated learning curve (change itself can be painful!). The surgeons who stayed with the traditional procedure believed that they could hold onto patients by selling them on the tried-and-true surgical approaches. Over time, more and more patients were asking for the new minimally invasive joint replacements and the traditional surgeons were increasingly feeling the pain of losing patients to their competitors that offered the new procedure.

While the learning curve for the new, minimally invasive procedure was perceived as "painful," it was even more painful losing patients and revenue. Sales professionals that offered to train these surgeons on the new surgical procedure offered a very compelling WIIFM.

The following list is in no way comprehensive, but gives several examples of points of "pain" that exist in medicine:

- Fear of harming the patient
- Fear of a poor result
- Time constraints of using certain products or procedures (procedures that take too long)
- Complex learning curves associated with new products and procedures
- Keeping up with competitive colleagues
- Cost of products and services
- Lack of reimbursement for certain products and services
- Need for additional profit centers in a physician's practice or hospital

- Satisfying the economic requirements at various institutions
- Conforming to accepted practice standards at the community and national level

Sales presentations must involve conversations that identify a problem, translate the problem into pain, and then aggravate the pain. The more the customer feels the pain, the more he or she will be open to a solution to solve it.

Let's look at another non-medical example. Let's say you live in Denver. It's July, the temperature outside is 85 degrees and you are buying tires for your car. The tire salesman asks, "Would you like to get a set of chains for your tires while you're here? You're subconscious is thinking, WIIFM? Snow is the furthest thing from your mind in this balmy weather, and you don't want to store them until winter. There's no reason to buy chains now. You'll just get them when the snow comes. No sale.

What if the tire salesman takes a different approach? Let's say he asks, "Sir, do you drive this car in the wintertime?"

You say, "Of course. It's the only car I have."

He asks, "Do you have a set of chains for this size tire?"

You reply, "No. I'll pick up a set at the first snow."

Up until this point, the salesman has identified the problem—you don't have any chains for your tires. But there is not sufficient pain for you to buy them now,(i.e., no snow). Let's see what happens when he introduces some pain.

The salesman says to you, "Sir, I don't know if you're aware, but we are expecting an extreme shortage of tire chains this year. The largest manufacturer of tire chains has closed two of three manufacturing plants due to the increased cost of raw materials. They have notified all of their retail outlets to expect severe tire chain shortages through February. Do you do any driving in the mountains, sir?"

You say, "Yes I do. We like to ski on weekends."

The salesman says, "As you know, it is illegal to drive on the mountain roads without tire chains in winter road conditions. How are you going to get to the slopes if you can't drive your car because you don't have chains?"

Suddenly you feel the pain of not being able to drive your car to go skiing on weekends, all because you waited too long to buy chains.

Now, the salesman decides to turn up the pain up a bit. He says, "The weather people are predicting record snowfall for this year. We're going to have the best skiing in the last 10 years, so you're going to be looking forward to jumping in the car and heading for the mountains. Come November, do you want to spend your time calling every tire store in the country looking for chains? I have a set of chains for your new tires in stock that I can package in a burlap bag and place them in your trunk, and in November, if you stop by with them, we'll put them on at no charge. Or, you can wait until November and try to find a set of chains."

Did you start to feel the pain of needing to take the time to shop around for tire chains? When you were just offered the solution, (i.e., the chains), the lack of pain did not make buying them a priority. However, once you felt the pain of needing to shop for them, and the greater pain of not being able to locate them, and the even greater pain of not being able to drive your car to go skiing—buying them now becomes an easy decision.

No problem, no pain, no sale. Always identify the problem before you try to solve it. If you want the prospect to be more open to your solution, stir up the pain a bit. We'll discuss this in more detail in the chapter on presentation skills.

Selling is Not a Monologue—It is a Conversation

Many people mistakenly believe that selling is nothing more than telling your prospects everything you know about your product or service and hoping that they will buy. It doesn't work that way. Effective selling requires an exchange of information. That means your prospects need to be "telling," also.

Medical professionals seldom have downtime during their work day. There is just too much to do and much to be concerned with. It's very easy for your prospects' minds to wander during your presentations unless they are actively involved. Some may allow you in the door and give you time to talk, but they are not fully listening to your sales presentation.

Often, when I would arrive for a sales call with surgeons in their offices, they would be busy reviewing patient's charts, dictating reports or consulting with colleagues on the telephone. Most were polite enough to give me their attention once they finished the current task, except for one surgeon who was determined to continue dictating his patient reports, even though I was sitting in front of him. I waited for Dr. Louis to take his head out of the charts, put down his Dictaphone and look at me. Finally, he said, "Mace, go ahead. I'm listening," as he continued to talk into the recorder. I sat quietly for a few seconds waiting for him to look up. He didn't! He said, "Are you just going to sit there, or do you have something to show me?"

I had no choice. I needed to start my presentation or leave. But, how could I engage a guy who wasn't even looking at me? I knew that if I did all the talking, it would be no different than talking to the wall. I just started asking him questions about how he performed the procedure where my product might be used. I made sure to ask open-ended questions that forced Dr. Louis to elaborate. I found out that he was somewhat cocky and liked to tout his approaches as being "the gold standard" in his specialty. He soon set his dictating machine down on his desk and became very involved in the conversation, and soon was telling me things I needed to know in order to sell him my product. Getting every prospect talking is the first step to a successful presentation.

Don't Use Your Salesperson Voice

One of the other keys I've learned over the years for keeping the prospect involved is to speak with him or her in the same voice I would use as if I were having a casual conversation with a friend. I think it's funny when I work with a salesperson in the classroom and then go on a sales call with him or her to witness a completely different personality. Some salespeople step into the "salesperson role" and their manner and voice changes. Be yourself! If you're excited about what you're selling, let it show in your voice and body, as if you were showing your product to your best friend. Don't fake it; just let it flow. That helps to create a conversation in which it is easier for the prospect to stay mentally and physically involved.

Plan Your Sales Presentation—Winging It is a Bad Idea

We are going to break the sales conversation down into several parts, and each part needs to be planned in advance. The best teams in sports are the best because they always have a game plan. You need to do the same. In the next sections on sales presentations, we'll discuss how to plan ahead for each part, so that you are able to move the sales process forward with each step.

11

Presentation Skills: Opening the Sales Conversation

It's 12:50 P.M. when you are escorted to Dr. Adams's office. He's finishing a sandwich at his desk while reviewing the charts of patients he will be seeing during his afternoon office hours. Dr. Adams starts seeing patients at 1 P.M.—you've got 10 minutes for your presentation. How will you begin?

Naturally, you'll start with a cordial greeting or a friendlier one, depending on the level of the relationship. If this is your first meeting, introduce yourself, even though the customer probably already knows who you, are by saying, "Good afternoon Dr. Adams. I'm Ted Alcott, with ABC Medical. I'm glad we both found the time to meet today." Notice that I did not say, "Doctor, thank you so much for taking some of your valuable time to meet with me today." Many salespeople diminish their value by suggesting that the customer's time is more valuable than their own. If your product or service can benefit the provider or the patient, they need to hear about it. They need you to inform them as much as you need them to listen. Be gracious, but don't diminish your own value.

Shaking hands in our society has become a standard of courtesy. Do what feels natural to you. I believe in waiting for the customer to extend his or her hand before offering mine—especially if he or she is eating at the time, as often happens during lunchtime sales calls. Some people are not very eager to shake hands with people they don't know, especially while consuming food. There is nothing wrong with offering your hand first, I just prefer to let the customer take the lead. And then, if you are going to shake hands—shake hands! A limp, wimpy handshake is not the way to make a good first impression. Deliver a firm handshake, but also avoid the "bone-crusher," especially with a woman. Also, many medical professionals, especially surgeons, are protective of their hands.

Get Down To Business—You're Not There to Visit

Many salespeople think it's important to establish rapport at the beginning of a sales presentation. That's a good idea, but the way to do it is not by talking about trivial, non-business related issues. Consider that you are sitting with a very busy professional and you have 10 minutes for your presentation to move the sales process forward. When you are calling on a doctor in his or her office, be aware that doctors often have a keen awareness of how valuable their office time is. This is where they earn their living. Let's say a doctor's practice grosses $500 per hour when he is seeing patients. If the doctor is spending 10 minutes with you, he or she is giving up $83 in practice income to speak with you. Think about the customer's WIIFM! Make it worth the doctor's time and money. Just because the doctor's office is full of golf knick-knacks does not mean that he wants to give up 10 minutes of his hourly income to discuss last year's Masters Golf Tournament! You could mention that you too, are an avid golfer, and that you would like to talk golf with him sometime, but you're here today to discuss something that's important to his practice and his patients.

Talking about common interests, however, is not the only way to establish rapport, and not even the best. Rapport begins with the customer having a good feeling about you as a professional. The bond of rapport is served when you show that you respect the customer's valuable time and his or her job as a healthcare provider. One of the best ways to build rapport is to show interest in the customer and the customer's world. You do this by getting them to talk about themselves and their world as you listen intently. This will build rapport way faster than talking about golf!

Another consideration is that you want to leave the door open to come back another time. It may take many sales calls before you can close the sale, and you want the customer to feel good about scheduling more time with you. He might not do that if he feels you spend too much time talking about non-practice-related issues. Besides, making something else a conversational priority diminishes the perceived value of your product or service. It can't be that great if you would rather discuss sports!

Selling time with a busy healthcare professional is like water in the desert—you wouldn't waste it on washing your hands. Use that time for your most essential purpose—selling! Healthcare professionals understand the value of time. Show them that you do too, by getting down to business immediately.

Don't Begin by Talking About Your Product; Talk About the Customer

Your opening must draw the prospect into the presentation. Let's talk about the little voice again. As you begin your presentation, the customer's little voice might be thinking, "Okay, Ted from ABC

Medical—what are you going to try to sell me today and will I be the least bit interested?" Basically the little voice is asking, "What's in it for me—WIIFM?" Your initial task is to engage him in a sales *conversation* that will answer that question.

Remember your position versus your customer's. You are a sales professional. The customer is a healthcare professional. While you may be the expert regarding your product or service, the customer is a true expert in his or her field. How do you think the customer feels when a salesperson tells him about things he already knows, being an expert? He may resent it.

Because your customer is the *expert* in his or her field, why not let them be the expert! In other words, don't tell an expert what he already knows. Get them to tell you. How? Ask the right questions!

One of the best ways to open a presentation is with a question. The question needs to relate to an issue or problem that does or may exist in the provider's practice. The purpose is to get the prospect to focus on the problem, or the pain. Of course, you must be prepared to offer a solution to this pain.

For example, if you were selling orthopedic implants used for total knee replacements, you might ask a surgeon, "Dr. Adams, what do you do when the correct anterior-posterior sized femoral component on a total knee has a lateral or medial overhang?" Sit back and let the doctor answer. You have just stepped into his world, and he is going to tell you about his experience with respect to your question and whether or not it has been an issue for him. He may elaborate regarding his philosophy regarding overhang and how to address it, or whether it should even be addressed. Or, he may tell you that he has never experienced an overhang and is not the least bit concerned about the issue. Don't you think these are important things to know before you offer a solution?

Allow the customer to say what he wants to say—never interrupt him—but don't let him go off on a tangent, either. Ask questions that will bring him back on track if necessary, and lead the conversation the way you need it to go. Of course, other areas of opportunity may come up during this discovery process, and you'll need to move in that direction if it makes more sense. Above all, make sure you keep the prospect focused on the problem you want to solve with your product or service.

How do you respond when a healthcare provider says, "I've never experienced that problem. I'm really not concerned about it?" That makes it hard to offer a solution. What he's telling you, in essence, is that he feels no pain regarding the issue. If this happens, you might try to *deliver the pain* by sharing a story about another healthcare provider's pain or a patient's pain. Remember, no problem—no pain—no sale.

Delivering Pain

So, when Dr. Adams says, "Ted, in the few instances when I have had an overhang during a total knee, it has never been an issue. I'm not concerned about it," instead of telling him why he should be concerned, tell him a story about a colleague.

It might go something like this: "Dr Adams, obviously you select the component size very carefully, and the few instances of overhang you experienced were not an issue for your patients. Nationally, surgeons around the country are telling a different story. One of the other surgeons in town told me about several patients who have had moderate to severe complications from the overhang with the knee system you are using. He told me about a patient who started having patella-tracking problems, and then the skin ulcerated in the area of the overhang and the knee got infected. The doctor removed the implants, but several months later, the knee was still infected and the poor patient had to have her leg amputated above the knee. Doctor, complications like that are pretty rare, aren't they?"

Dr. Adams would probably answer, "Yes. Infections that don't respond to treatment are rare."

You now have a chance to get him to own the possibility of it happening. "Dr. Adams, is it true that any time the skin is compromised around a total knee, infection is a possibility?"

Dr. Adams might respond, "Sure, it's a possibility, but severe infections such as you described are rare."

You continue, "Thank heaven that severe infections like that are uncommon. You know what surprised me and most of the surgeons I have spoken with? A recent multi-center study published in The Journal showed that medial or lateral overhang occurs up to 14 percent of the time with some knee systems. XYZ medical thought it was important to address the problem, and if it's okay, I'd like to show you how we can help you avoid ever having to deal with a complication like that other surgeon did. Would that be alright?"

I just gave you an example to show how you might be able to create some pain even when the prospect isn't feeling any. A story allows you to share the pain without your trying to tell the expert what he or she should be doing. You do this by telling a story about how another expert had to deal with a similar situation.

Don't sensationalize the story, it needs to be real and documentable. If you have an article in a peer review journal or some other third party reference, use it for support.

Hopefully, you see the value of opening your presentation with a conversation that gets your prospect to identify or acknowledge a problem and some level of associated pain. If you do what an unfortunate majority of sales representatives do and just start talking about solutions, your prospect's little voice might just be saying: "This is a waste of time! I don't have this problem. I need to get rid of this sales rep as soon as possible!"

A rookie sales representative often begins a sales presentation by talking about his product, while the medical sales professional talks about the healthcare provider and his or her world first, with a clear focus on a problem, before offering a solution.

In the next chapter, I will show you how to get more involved in connecting the prospect with the problem. Remember what you need to do when you open a sales presentation:

Let your prospects know what is in it for them (WIIFM),
and why it is worth their time to pay attention.

12

Presentation Skills: Asking Healthcare Professionals the Right Questions

Good salespeople know how to use questions to create the sales conversation. Effective questioning skills are especially important in healthcare sales, because the customer is often an expert in some area of patient care. Healthcare providers may resent it if you, as a salesperson, try to educate them about their area of expertise, as they naturally presume their level of knowledge is much higher than yours. When you merely tell them that your product or service is a better way of treating their patients, you lose credibility in the customer's eyes, because you have a conflict of interest, in that you will benefit financially if they buy your product. However, while these experts may not respond well to a salesperson telling them what they should or should not be doing in their practice, or how good their product or service is, they almost never object to appropriate questions.

Salespeople know that they should be asking questions in their presentations, and most think they are doing it effectively. When I facilitate my live "Success Skills for Medical Sales Professionals" workshop, I always ask how many of the medical salespeople in the room use questions in their sales presentations. Almost everyone's hand goes up.

I will ask for a volunteer to come up and demonstrate one of his or her sales presentations, and the participant might ask one or two generic questions in a role play, but often, the presentation is just a re- gurgitation of the details of the product. Frequently, the only ques- tion the salesperson asks is, "Would you like to try it?" which is supposed to be a close, albeit it a weak one.

The truth is that not everyone uses questions effectively. Let's begin with an understanding of what effective questioning is and what it is not.

What Questioning Is

Effective questioning serves three purposes during a sales presentation:

- It keeps the prospect involved in the presentation
- It reveals information
- It helps you to control the conversation and keep it moving in a di- rection that can lead to a sale

Keep the Prospect Involved in the Sales Conversation

The busy medical professionals you sell to have a lot going on in their heads. They are often dealing with patient issues that are more pressing than the new widget you want to show them. If they are not actively participating in the sales conversation, there is a good chance that their thoughts are somewhere else. It is not unusual for a healthcare prospect to sit back and allow a salesperson to droll on endlessly about a prod- uct or service without the prospect ever saying a word. Questions pull the prospect into the conversation and help hold their attention.

A question can instantly change one's focus. No one can answer a question without hearing what was asked. Even a busy healthcare professional won't blow off an appropriate question because, doing so would be rude, and most people don't want to be perceived as such. Because your prospect must hear your question to answer it, he or she will usually ask you to repeat the question if they weren't listening, so they can respond. Good questions keep the prospect involved.

Find Out What You Need To Know

Selling is not telling, but without discovering your prospects concerns and issues, you are limited to talking about your product and at best, guessing what those issues and concerns might be. Why guess? Ask!

Sales professionals are told to think of themselves as consultants, (i.e. bearers of solutions). How can you possibly propose your product or service as a solution without thoroughly understanding the customer's perception of the problem? Don't wait for the prospect to volunteer the information—ask what you need to know.

Questions Allow the Experts to be Experts

Remember that healthcare professionals are the experts in their field. Many salespeople try to demonstrate how much they know, in the hopes that it will impress the prospect, but showing off how knowledgeable you are won't necessarily increase your chances of doing business. In fact, some medical professionals enjoy an opportunity to show how little a salesperson knows. It's much easier to let the experts be experts. How? By asking questions that prompt the prospect to make the point that you wish to make!

Telling a healthcare provider what's right, what they should do or how to do it can be a recipe for disaster. Consider posing any statement that you would like to make as a question, because that offers an opportunity for discussion without seeming like you are suggesting that you know more than the customer about a given issue.

Say, for example, that you want to sell an X-ray machine that reduces patient radiation exposure. You are having a sales conversation with Barbara, the chief radiology technologist at a hospital, and you say, "Your current X-ray machine produces a high level of radiation that may be detrimental to the patient." Think about how this might be interpreted. Barbara may construe your statement to imply that she is ignorant of the radiation risks posed by the equipment that she has been using for the last 10 years. Or, she may think that you are implying that she *doesn't care* about the possibility of detrimental effects. Perhaps she just might resent a salesperson telling her what she obviously needs to know to do her job.

You could make the point by using a question that doesn't have any of these implications by saying, "Barbara, our XR282 machine produces 40 percent less X-ray exposure than any machine manufactured before 2005. How might this benefit your department and your patients?"

Barbara might reply, "Wow! That's a significant reduction in X-ray exposure to my staff and the patient." See the difference when she says it, compared to when you say it? Of course! If you say it, she can doubt it, but if she says it, then to her, it's true! Let the expert be the expert.

But, what happens if Barbara were to answer, "X-ray exposure is not a factor in my department?"

Some sales reps might instantly respond by citing studies and data to prove that she is wrong: "Barbara, a 1999 study performed at XYZ Medical Center proved unequivocally that radiation exposure can increase the morbidity of patients with certain diseases." That's almost the same as saying, "Barbara, you're wrong. Don't you keep up with the latest studies?" That's the way your scientific paper citation might sound to her. If you make her feel stupid, do you think she will want to buy from you?

When Barbara says, "X-ray exposure is not a factor in my department," you could respond, "Barbara, tell me how you manage exposure in your department." You have just placed her in control as the authority in her world. She will tell you all the ways that her department minimizes exposure and why she doesn't feel that your machine's lower radiation exposure is a benefit. You're learning information you need to know now that you will address later as objections. We'll cover objections in another chapter.

You Must Control the Conversation

Healthcare professionals are used to having some level of control regarding patient treatments, the people that report to them and yes, even you—the medical sales representative. Because they often call the shots, taking control is natural for them. These professionals can hijack your sales presentation and use it to sound off about a troubling issue that is unrelated to your product or service, or to ramble about other issues that won't help your sale. You need to be able to keep them on a path that will advance the sale without them feeling that you're being pushy. Questions allow you to do this.

What do you do when a customer goes off on a tangent or is discussing something other than what you wish to discuss? Ask a question to change the focus. Let's say that you ask Mrs. Smith about the hospital's budget for new infection control devices. She begins to answer, but then starts to talk about how today's staff is more interested in personal benefits programs, time off, etc. Clearly, the information is not helping your sale. How do you get back to the budget issue in a comfortable way? Wait for the prospect to pause and ask, "Mrs. Smith, I'm curious. You were saying a moment ago that infection control has a discretionary budget. How does that money get allocated?" Voila! You're back on track, by gently redirecting the conversation with a question.

The control of the conversation can shift many times during a sales presentation. The last person asking a question is in control. Suppose you're talking about your X-ray machine with Barbara and she asks you a question, taking control of the conversation with a less-than-friendly tone. How do you answer her question and regain control? If Barbara says, "Tom, do you think that radiation exposure is the only thing that I have to worry about in this department? The image quality and the budget are important factors, as well. I'm concerned about exposure, but we need to have good images, too. Do you think that you can sell me your X-ray machine just because it produces less radiation?"

Notice that Barbara is now in control. You want to be polite and answer her question, but you also want to recapture control and return the conversation to a positive tone as soon as possible. You might respond, "Barbara, of course not. I know you have many issues that you need to be concerned about. Tell me about your image quality requirements (or your budgetary requirements)." You're back in control and about to receive more valuable information.

Beyond getting information, you are also demonstrating a concern for the prospect's issues. It's insulting to a medical professional for you to walk in and attempt to sell your product without taking the time to understand his or her situation. Once they trust that you understand their problems, they will be more open to learning about your solutions.

What Questioning Is Not

It is important to realize that questioning, as I'm describing it here, is intended to be part of a conversation, not an interrogation. The questions must seem natural and appropriate to the discussion. Your goal is not to face down your prospect with question after question until they agree to buy, but to clarify the information that is important to the sale.

Questioning is intended to get information, not as a method to impose your opinion. When questioning is done in a way that suggests impatience or disagreement, it is no different than making a statement of a similar nature. Your questions must be conversational, or you are defeating their purpose.

Types of Questions

There are basically two types of questions: *closed-ended questions and open-ended questions.*

It is my experience that most salespeople use closed-ended questions; those that can be simply answered with a yes or no. These questions are usually used when a salesperson is seeking to tie down a statement. For example, "Radiation exposure is something that all X-ray employees are concerned about, isn't that true?"

Open-ended questions require a more elaborate response and cannot be answered with just one syllable. Open-ended questions are best for obtaining useful information, and begin with the words who, what, where, when, why and how. Alternatively, you can also use a phrase like, "Tell me about . . ." Open-ended questions get your prospect talking, while affording you the opportunity to sit back, listen and learn.

Another important benefit of open-ended questions is that it's easier to sense the customer's emotion in the ensuing answer, as compared to a simple yes or no. This is beneficial, because buying decisions are often based on emotion.

To summarize, let's take a look at how questions are used to get to the point of presenting data about your product or service.

Use Questions to Identify the Problem and Stir Up the Pain

We've talked about the importance of clearly identifying a problem that you can solve before offering a solution. We also know that the more pain a customer feels with respect to the problem, the more open he or she will be to hearing about solutions.

Questions are the best way to identify problems and pain. If *you tell* a healthcare customer that there is a problem, he or she can doubt you. When *they state* the problem, they are certain that there *is a problem*!

Notice the following sequence in questioning:

- Ask questions to get the customer to state the problem
- Ask questions to get the customer to discuss the effects the problem has on the patient, the customer, or the customer's practice or employer
- Ask questions that get the customer to describe how he and the patient might benefit by solving the problem

Here's how it might sound in a sales conversation between a medical sales professional and a surgeon discussing total hip replacement surgery. The sales professional wants to get the doctor to consider a device for assessing leg lengths prior to and after replacing the hip:

"Doctor, how do you determine your leg lengths, both before and after the femoral neck osteotomy (cutting off the ball of the femur)?"

"I measure the distance from the iliac crest to the tip of the greater trochanter, then I cut a finger breadth above the lesser trochanter."

"Have you ever had a problem with unequal leg lengths?"

"Of course I have. It's one of the risks of the procedure. I tell all my patients that it's a possibility before the surgery when I'm going over complications."

"What kinds of problems have you seen in patients with unequal leg lengths following total hip replacement?"

"Some patients have an altered gait or limp. In more severe cases, some patients have some weakness flexing or extending the hip."

"What problems are associated with the weakness you mentioned?"

"Patients might have problems getting out of a chair, climbing stairs or even walking. Fortunately, it does not happen very often."

"That's good! So, how would the patient benefit if there was a way to consistently create equal leg lengths?"

"The patient would get a better result, with better muscle performance, no limp and a normal gait. Overall, the patient would just be happier. But getting the leg lengths equal all the time is pretty hard to do. Do you have something that will allow me to do this?"

"Doctor, I believe I have the solution you're looking for . . ."

Let's review the information that was revealed through the use of questions and the sequence:

- The problem: unequal leg lengths
- Effect of problem: altered gait, limp, weakness in flexing and extending the hip joint; difficulty getting out of chairs, climbing stairs and walking
- Benefit of solving problem: better results for patient, no limp, good muscle function and happier patients

The customer has stated the problems and pain associated with the problem. He has also stated the benefit of solving the problem. You have a customer who should be more open to hearing your solution now, because he has helped you to "build the case" for your product.

Warning: Avoid Asking Accusatory Questions

I have discovered over the years that one of the worst questions a medical salesperson can ask a healthcare provider is one that suggests the prospect has problems or challenges in his or her practice. Keep in mind that healthcare providers are generally content with the way they do what they do. Among other things, the ego helps to support the "Things are fine," position. As a result, they may resent you "accusing" them of having problems or challenging them directly.

What do I mean? Inexperienced salespeople sometimes ask questions that are too general, such as, "Doctor, what problems do you encounter when you perform colonoscopies?"

What is wrong with this question? The salesperson has a product that can solve a problem. Therefore, the customer must have a problem. The sales person is trying to get the customer to reveal that problem.

How do many healthcare customers respond to a general question such as, "What problems or challenges do you have?" They respond, "I don't have any problems. I have been doing this for years. I know what I'm doing. Everything is fine." Remember, in most customers' minds, they are treating their patients effectively. How dare some salesperson come in here and suggest otherwise?

How can you avoid accusing your customers of having problems and challenges? Don't ask overly general questions. Make your questions specific, or credit the problem to the customer's colleagues. For example, don't ask, "Doctor, what are your challenges when performing colonoscopies," because it is too general—he performs colonoscopies every day and doesn't perceive any real problems. Also, don't ask, "Doctor, how do you deal with the problem of X," in which the doctor may feel like you are accusing him of having that problem, which he may resent.

Instead, reference the problems to his colleagues that perform colonoscopies. "Doctor, gastroenterologists report adequate distension as a potential problem with colonoscopies. What is your experience and thoughts about that?" The doctor will tell you his experience and thoughts because you asked, and because you did not accuse him of having the problem. This also shows that you respect the customer as an expert, which serves to drive the flow of information you need.

Start Winning with Questions

You cannot predict with any certainty exactly how any conversation will go. Generally speaking, using skilled questions allows you to control the conversation and get the customer to state what's important to him or her. Even if the conversation doesn't go exactly as planned, you will be uncovering valuable information you can use to either close the sale or eliminate the healthcare provider as a prospect for your product or service.

The most successful medical sales professionals know how to use questions to:

- Get information
- Keep the prospect engaged in the conversation
- Stay in control
- Let the expert to be the expert

It has been said that a good salesperson listens more than he speaks.

This requires that you get the prospect talking, specifically, about what you need to know. If you find yourself doing most of the talking during a sales conversation, you need ask more questions.

Mastering the use of questions is a major step toward mastering medical sales.

13

Presentation Skills: Presenting Solutions

Showing the customer how your product or service can solve his problem seems easy. To the untrained, it appears that selling is nothing more than telling the customer all the details about your product, with the expectation that the customer will buy. This is what is known as a "data dump," and reflects the sales skills of an amateur.

There are many problems with simply dumping product information on your prospect. For one thing, you risk losing the prospect's attention. You could find yourself ecstatically expounding on how your product is going to deliver desired outcomes while the prospect is thinking about how he can finish his office hours by 4:30. When this happens, you are presenting data to no one but yourself.

Another problem with this "show up and throw up" approach is that you may be offering solutions that do not key in on any of your prospect's concerns or problems. Intuitively, it would seem that if you just throw all the product benefits on the table, then the prospect will identify one or more that he likes. That might happen, but realistically, with most of the points you're presenting, the customer's little voice is saying, "My current product does that. I don't have a problem.

I don't see the difference between what you have and what I'm already using." These are *objections*, and you're the one who is creating them!

Remember, while you are operating from an excitement of gain perspective, your healthcare customer is often operating from a fear of loss point of view. In other words, you are blissfully spewing details about your product while your prospect is looking for a way to shoot you down. Don't help him by reciting everything you know. The last chapter discussed using effective questioning to focus in on the customer's key issues and associated pain. Why make assumptions during the sales process, when some simple questions will tell you the features of your product that the prospect will be most interested in.

As we move forward from this point, let's assume that you have asked the right questions and you have identified the customer's issues and concerns. The remainder of this chapter will focus on delivering the solution that you have crafted to suit your customer's needs.

Emphasize the Benefits that Solve the Prospect's Problems

Suppose that your company just released a new widget that has won all kinds of design awards. You have four color promotional pieces that talk about the great lines of the design, the reduced weight of the widget, and its high-tech, stainless steel appearance. You are excited about these features and you think your prospects will be excited about them, too. Before you move forward with product presentations, ask yourself this question: What are the benefits to the user and his patients?

Healthcare providers might agree that a product has a cool feature, but realistically, they want to know what's in it for them (WIIFM) and their patients (WIIFMP). Every statement you make when you are delivering data needs to answer these questions.

Talking about features and benefits might seem rudimentary but it is important that you discuss both during your sales presentations.

Describing a *feature* tells the customer how your product looks, feels or operates. Features by themselves do not sell products, because they do not answer the questions WIIFM or WIIFMP. For example, the ergonomically designed handle of your surgical instrument might look good, and the word *ergonomically* sounds impressive. Does that alone allow the prospect to answer the question—WIIFM?

When you describe a *benefit,* you are describing the results or outcomes that the feature provides for the healthcare provider or his patient. The benefit is the answer to WIIFM or WIIFMP. Your customers don't buy features; they buy benefits that solve their problems and eliminate their pain. When you describe a feature of your product to a customer, don't leave him hanging on the WIIFM question by failing to describe how it will benefit him and his patients. For example, if you showed a customer that your new surgical instrument has an ergonomically designed handle, you would also explain the benefit: *"You'll notice that the instrument's handle has an ergonomic design* [The Feature]. *This reduces hand fatigue for the surgeon and minimizes excision of healthy tissue* [The Benefit]."

"So What?"

When you are preparing for your sales presentation, which is a must, you can test your product information statements to make sure that they pass the "So what?" test. Ask yourself whether or not your prospect's little voice can justifiably say *"So what?"* when you deliver the information. Using our previous example, if you just tell a customer that your new instrument has an ergonomically designed handle, he might say "So what?" which fits, because the ergonomically designed *feature* does not mean anything by itself. If "So what?" fits, your statement fails the test.

Now try the "So what?" test when you add the benefit statement to the feature. "*This reduces hand fatigue for the surgeon and minimizes excision of healthy tissue.*" Can your customer's little voice say "So what?" to that? Probably not, because hand fatigue and harming healthy tissue are important issues for a surgeon. Your statement now passes the "So what?" test!

Why Not Lead with the Benefits?

You hopefully can see why you lose some sales impact when you describe a feature without discussing the benefit. Customers don't buy a product or service for its features; they buy because of the product's or service's benefits, (i.e. the ability of a product or service to produce a desired outcome, solve an existing problem or remove some level of associated pain.

Here is something to consider. Because customers buy benefits, *why not lead with benefits* during your sales presentations? Talk about the problem, the pain associated with the problem and how your product solves that problem *before showing the feature that yields the desired benefit*. It reverses the way most salespeople make their presentations and allows you to take control of the little voice. Let me show you what this might look like, using our surgical instrument example. It starts by exposing the problem and the associated pain.

"Dr. Smith, the surgeons that perform the Mitrumpi procedure often state that the preservation of healthy tissue as one of their biggest challenges. They describe the inability to effectively limit the movement at the cutting end of the instrument as what compromises the healthy tissue, and many have suggested that surgeon hand fatigue is a contributing factor to the unwanted movement at the tip. What has been your experience?"

"No question. The Mitrumpi is a long procedure, and it doesn't take long for my hand to start cramping up. Even without the fatigue issue, it's difficult to keep that tip where you want it every time you resect some tissue."

"What problems are associated with resecting healthy tissue?"

"Two problems, mainly . . . the first is that the surrounding tissue itself is weakened, and the second is that it takes longer to heal."

"Is the hand fatigue an issue for you?"

"I deal with it, but sometimes my hand and forearm are sore for the rest of the day after I do that procedure. It would be nice if there was a better way . . ."

"Dr. Smith, XYZ Medical has redesigned the instrument to eliminate hand fatigue and minimize trauma to surrounding, non-targeted tissue. The tip remains where you want it, and hand fatigue is eliminated. This was done by using an ergonomically designed handle. Here, try out the mechanism . . ."

Did you notice the sequence? First, the salesperson introduced the problems described by the doctor's colleagues, instead of asking, "What are your problems . . . ?" Next, he sought the doctor's feelings regarding the shared information. When the doctor showed agreement that a problem existed, the salesperson stirred the pain by asking the doctor to describe the consequences of removing excess tissue and sought confirmation about the fatigue issue. Next, the salesperson described the benefit of the new instrument and finally, the feature that created it.

Isn't that approach more effective than, "Doctor, we've redesigned the instrument with an ergonomically designed handle. What do you think?"

Always State the Benefit

Never assume that your prospect knows the benefit of your product's features. Always tie each feature to one or more benefits.

Medical sales reps who sometimes leave out discussing benefits may do so with the feeling that the benefit is obvious and that stating it to the prospect may seem insulting. Prefacing the statement with a simple "of course" can mitigate this, by suggesting that the prospect, "of course," knows this. For example, if you are concerned that the benefit of your ergonomically designed handle is obvious and stating the benefit may offend your prospect, you can instead say, " and of course, this obviously provides you with better control of instrument placement, with reduced trauma to the surrounding tissue."

Don't Talk about All of the Product's Features and Benefits

The only features and benefits worth talking about are those that the prospect will buy because they solve a perceived problem or pain. Too many salespeople feel the need to rattle off all of the features and benefits of a product that their company probably provided in a neat list somewhere. If you do this, you may be working against the sale.

The number one reason for objections in sales is offering too many benefits! What is the problem with too many benefits? The prospect perceives that you're trying to solve problems he doesn't have.

Each unwanted feature has the little voice saying, "I don't need that." The subtotal of a bunch of "I don't need that" statements is the prospect's perception that he or she does not need your product or service. Stick to discussing the benefits that solve the problem or pain.

Check In With the Prospect

It is very easy for sales presentations to become one-sided with the salesperson doing all the talking, and the result may be the loss of your prospect's attention. If the prospect is not actively participating in your presentation, you need to periodically check in. Checking in is nothing more than asking a question to assess your prospect's thoughts at a given point.

Let's suppose that you just delivered a feature/benefits statement to your prospect. You could check in with him by asking a simple question, such as, "Would that be a benefit to you with respect to the way that you perform the procedure?" If your prospect's attention has drifted, he will need to refocus to answer your question.

You can also check in with your prospect before delivering the features/benefits statement. For example, "Dr. Smith, have you ever noticed how the starting torque on a drill can cause the tip to migrate into the soft tissue?" When the prospect answers, "Yes," you can proceed to describe your features and benefits, knowing that you have his attention.

Unless your prospect interacts with you throughout the presentation, you need check in at least once or twice each minute. Don't assume that the prospect is hearing what you are saying just because you are talking and he is looking in your direction.

Tell a Story

One of the best ways to demonstrate a benefit while keeping the prospect's attention is to use a story. It is very difficult for a prospect to not listen to a story, especially if it involves a situation with one of his colleagues, or describes something similar to his own experience.

Your story can be as simple as the following: "I had the new suture passer at a surgery for one of my surgeons recently. He had not performed an endoscopic procedure in almost a year, yet it took him less than one minute to pass the suture through the hole in the radius. Your P.A., Paul, mentioned that you perform these procedures fairly regularly. How much time might this instrument save you on your cases?"

Stories are a very effective way to describe the capabilities of your product or service. Healthcare professionals often say that they don't place much credence in anecdotal medicine, but they will still listen to a story that keeps them mentally involved as they learn about your product or service.

There are a few things to keep in mind when using stories in your sales presentations.

The stories must be real. Your prospect may check your story out or discover any conflicting details by accident. If the details of the story are other than the way that you described them, you will lose credibility.

When telling stories, you need to protect the privacy of the people and institutions in your story. This means not naming a healthcare professional, patient or institution, unless you have obtained permission. This holds true even when your story portrays the characters in a positive light. You want all of your prospects and customers to know that they respect the privacy of everyone, so that they will never feel vulnerable by sharing information with you or allowing you to serve them or their patients. You may use names of professionals that have published data in scientific journals only when you are referencing those published articles.

When you refer to another healthcare professional as a satisfied customer, make sure you have obtained permission from that person first.

Also, be reasonably certain that the person you are using as a reference is highly regarded by the prospect. Otherwise, you might hear, "Well, if that guy is using your product, I won't!"

Visual Aids Can Help or Hinder Your Presentation

The chances are that you use visual aids in your presentations because they have a dramatic impact. A picture or a demonstration is worth at least a thousand words. Use them effectively and visual aids can increase your chances of making the sale, but the opposite is also true—used carelessly, visual aids can be distracting, send the wrong message, confuse your prospect and kill your presentation.

Medical sales professionals routinely use the following visual aids: product samples, brochures, charts, surgical technique monographs, PowerPoint presentations, video clips, anatomical models, product prototypes and others. Each has distinct uses in advancing the sale. I want to talk about using visual aids in general as another tool to keep the prospect involved and how to avoid some potential problems.

One problem is that you can become so engrossed in a visual aid that it fuels a big data dump. Many medical sales representatives get excited when they are showing and describing a new product to a customer, and it is easy to get carried away if you don't stay focused on the two or three important points that are solutions to the prospect's specific problems.

Medical professionals tend to be visual and kinesthetic. They don't want to just hear about your product, they want to hold it, examine it and assess it from an ergonomic perspective. On one hand, this is good, because it gets the prospect intimately involved with the product. On the other hand, it is dangerous, because you can lose control of the visual aid and your sales presentation. If the prospect is engrossed in a visual aid, he might not be paying attention to a word you're saying. So, while it is good to give the prospect *temporary* control of a visual aid, you must know how to take control back.

If you want a prospect to handle a sample or look at it more closely, just say, "Here," and hand it over. Point out what you want them to feel, notice or examine, and ask for immediate feedback. This provides for a high level of involvement in the sales conversation. Getting the prospect involved this way is easy. I don't remember ever handing a visual aid to a prospect when they declined to take it.

What happens when you want to shift gears and talk about something else in the presentation, but the prospect is still looking at or playing with your visual aid? You have two choices. You can wait until the prospect is done looking at the visual aid and hands it back, or you can ask for it back. Regaining control is as simple as asking the prospect to hand you the visual aid so that you can demonstrate or point out something else. For example, you might say, "Dr. Conners, please hand me the drill for a moment. There's something important that I want to point out to you." Invariably, your prospect will hand it over. You can make quick reference to the visual aid and hand it back, or set it aside, saying, "I'll give this back to you shortly. I want to ask you about . . ." and then move on. You have regained control of the visual aid and the presentation.

Maintaining control of visual aids is important, regardless of the type you are using. I accompanied Phil, a relatively new sales representative, on a call to Mr. Roberts, the CEO of a hospital. Phil had prepared an impressive, 30-slide PowerPoint presentation on how his company could save the hospital money. Phil placed his laptop computer on the corner of the CEO's desk and started to go through his presentation. While Phil was explaining a slide, the CEO motioned for Phil to move his laptop closer and said, "Can I see your computer for a second?"

Phil said, "Sure," and slid it over to Mr. Roberts. The CEO placed the laptop squarely in front of him and then quickly paged through all 30 slides of the PowerPoint presentation in about a minute, ignoring Phil's request to wait.

The CEO looked up at Phil and said, "I've seen your presentation. I'm not interested. Thanks for coming by."

I was flabbergasted! I had never seen a presentation get hijacked like this (or met a more rude prospect!). Both Phil and I learned a huge lesson—never relinquish control of your visual aids, unless you are certain that you will be able to regain control. If a prospect tries to take control of a visual aid while you are in the middle of using it, politely tell him that you will be happy to let him examine it as soon as you are finished making your point, or once you complete the presentation.

The same thing can happen when you hand a prospect a product brochure. You're using the brochure to make a point, and the next thing you know, the prospect is paging through the brochure instead of listening to you. Don't let this happen! When you are using a brochure to demonstrate a point or show a picture, maintain control of the brochure by holding it in your hands as you point to the appropriate information. If the prospect asks if he can have a closer look, by all means bring the brochure closer, but hold onto it, if possible. If you need to relinquish the brochure to your prospect and then need to get it back, handle the situation the same as I described for getting back a product sample: "Dr. Smith, could you hand me the brochure for a second? There is something that I want to point out." Turn the page if you need to, make a reference, and set the brochure aside by saying, "I will leave this with you when we're done today."

What if a prospect insists on paging through a brochure or examining a product? By all means, let him! Beware that anything you say during their perusal might not be heard. If a prospect tells you to continue while he is paging through the information, politely tell him that you don't mind waiting until he is finished looking. This sends the message that you are not going to talk while the prospect is distracted by the visual aid.

Presenting Scientific Data

Using scientific data to support your claims during a presentation can be powerful. Healthcare professionals have been taught that all products and procedures should be supported by good science. Hence, it is often to your benefit to use scientific citations whenever they are available and appropriate.

The data in a scientific study is objective, (i.e. it is a collection of observations, measurements, etc.) However, data is subject to interpretation, and you need to show how the data supports using your product.

Here are some basic rules for using scientific papers to support your sales efforts:

1. Before you use a supporting article, *make sure you read it*. Some sales reps never read the article and just parrot what their company suggests the study implies. If a customer attempts to discuss the paper with you and you have not read it, you may seem incompetent and lose credibility. Read the paper, or don't use it!

2. Make sure you understand the article. Unless you have experience reading and interpreting scientific papers, ask a professional or colleague what the paper concludes or infers. If your company

sends you a copy of a paper without an explanation of how to use it, contact someone at the company for clarification. Sometimes, the true significance of a scientific study as it relates to your sales effort is not obvious.

3. Don't use the scientific paper to shove the information down your prospect's throat. If the customer or prospect disagrees with the study or your interpretation of the study, use that as a point of discussion to uncover any possible concerns or issues that the prospect may have. Don't try to use it as an instrument to prove the prospect is uninformed or mistaken. Suggesting to a medical professional that he or she is wrong does little to build rapport and advance the sale.

4. Never try to twist the content of a scientific paper into saying something that it really doesn't. For example, a particular study may state that, "the new device appears to offer several advantages over other similar devices currently available." Do not twist that erroneously into, "This study shows that our new device is superior to anything else on the market." That is a misstatement that could cost you your reputation. It also makes you seem like a stereotypical salesperson, out for your own benefit, instead of fostering a relationship in which you are considered a trusted consultant.

5. Do not get into a debate about the validity of a study or the credibility of the author with your customers. The prospect is entitled to his opinion and it is not your job to tell the prospect how he should interpret scientific data. You can share other clinician's interpretation of the results, but don't get into a debate. Remember, your customer likely perceives himself as more of the expert than you. If necessary, arrange for a legitimate expert, such as one of

your prospect's colleagues, to discuss any contentious issues with the prospect. This is preferable to attempting to overrule someone who may resent it.

Presenting Product Data Is Important, But There's More for You to Do

Hopefully, you see that presenting product data during a sales presentation is only one step in the sales process. You must be able to do it well, but you could be wasting your time if you don't clearly identify and discuss the problems to which your product is the solution first.

Remember, *selling is not telling*. It is an exchange of information in which you position your product or service as a reasonable solution to a problem or situation. Don't try to "wing it"—you must be prepared.

Medical sales professionals plan their data presentations *in detail* every time.

14

Selling Skills: Handling Objections

Nothing strikes fear in the hearts of some medical sales representatives like objections! But, receiving objections from those who are experts in their field is only frightening if you're not prepared. Once you know the process and properly prepare for each presentation, objections will be a welcome part of your presentations, well . . . most of the time.

What is an objection?

An objection is a question or statement made by a customer or prospect that reveals something that he or she disagrees with, has negative feelings about or does not believe to be accurate or true. Any other reason why the prospect is unable to proceed with the sale should also be considered an objection.

Contrary to the beliefs of some salespeople, an objection is not a fatal blow. Fledgling sales representatives sometimes expect a sales presentation to run like a carefully choreographed Broadway show—I say this. The customer says that. And then, at the conclusion, the customer says, "I'll take it." If only the customer had read the script! It just doesn't work that way. While you're helping the customer to realize all of the reasons he should buy, he is assembling his list of reasons why he shouldn't—objections!

Objections, and dealing with them, are a necessary part of the sales process. In fact, a presentation that is not interrupted by at least a few objections probably won't go anywhere, because objections tell you what is on the prospect's mind and keep the sales process moving forward.

Objections are good! They show that the prospect is paying attention to your presentation and has some level of interest. Objections provide you with the opportunity to clear up confusion or misinformation and bring the presentation back on track. Objections are the equivalent of a painful symptom that may signal a medical condition. While most people don't enjoy pain, intellectually, they recognize that many medical conditions would go undiagnosed without it.

The only time that objections are not good is when you are getting too many. This usually results from being unprepared, misstating information or touting benefits as solutions to problems that don't exist in your prospects' minds. Most objections can be handled, and many can be prevented with good preparation and planning.

The Problems That Sales People Have With Objections

Salespeople sometimes take objections personally. They feel that if a prospect or customer expresses negative beliefs or feelings about the salesperson's product or service during the sales process, then something is wrong with the presentation, the product, service or their company. These feelings start to create negative emotions that can snowball and destroy the salesperson's confidence.

Typical negative emotions that might result from a failure to handle objections include:

- I can't sell!
- My company's products are not as good as XYZ Company's
- This prospect is stupid and just doesn't *get it*
- My company has not provided adequate training
- I can't handle objections with medical professionals—they know way more than I do!

Negative emotions regarding objections often result from the salesperson's misinterpretation of what an objection really is. It's easy to misconstrue an objection as a prospect's dismissal of your product or service, but here is an important truth about objections.

An objection is not a rejection

An *objection*, again, reflects the prospect's beliefs, feelings, or opinion about your product or something you discussed. A *rejection* is a "true No," to your offering. Unless you have:

- Completely familiarized your prospect with the product or service
- Explained how its design specifically serves the both the doctor and his patients
- Fully and completely responded to all questions and concerns you should not consider any "No" as a final "No." In fact, unless your prospect says, "I won't use it," and has given you clear reasons that you cannot overcome, you have not been rejected.

Don't Make the Customer Wrong When Handling Objections

We all like to be right, especially when the sale is on the line. Too many medical sales representatives jump on the customer as soon as they hear an objection they know how to handle. Don't do this! Let's look at an example where Ted, a novice medical sales professional, is presenting information to Dr. Jones to get him to consider updating his old X-ray machine to a digital X-ray system.

"... and as you can see Dr. Jones, the image quality is excellent and ..."

"Ted, I've got to tell you. I'm happy with the image quality on my old X-ray machine. I don't see any advantages with your fancy, expensive digital machine."

"Dr. Jones, I have sample images here that clearly demonstrate that the new digital system can render far more detail than your old film cassette system. You could be missing important diagnostic details."

"Are you telling me how I should be practicing medicine?"

"Of course not, but if you want to offer your patient state-of-the-art diagnostics, you'll need to step up to newer technology."

"So now you're telling me that I'm not providing modern care for my patients. Tell me about your qualifications to judge me as a physician. Show me your medical degree!"

This is a worst-case scenario, in which a sales rep says something seemingly innocent and true, yet it is misinterpreted to mean something else. It is important to remember that doctors and other healthcare professionals are the experts. A prospect's objection represents his or her point of view and you don't have the same credentials. Whether a statement is correct or not, allow the prospect his or her point of view. If you just jump right in and attempt to correct the information, what have you done? You have essentially said, "You're wrong!"

It is human nature and part of our culture to respond to inaccurate information by correcting it immediately. We learned this as children. If we said something incorrect in school, the teacher would often correct us, or at least tell us we were wrong, right away. As a consequence of this, some sales reps do the same thing with customers, and it is not a good practice.

It is almost a reflex to correct erroneous information as soon as one hears it, with the intention of keeping the sales process moving forward, but it actually creates a schism between you and your prospect. Again, consider the ego of the healthcare professional—the one who perceives himself as the expert. He has the credentials. When you imply that your prospect is *wrong*, he may resent it.

Think about how an immediate answer to an objection might sound to the prospect. Suppose they raise an objection and you just jump right in and correct them. For example, if a prospective customer tells you he doesn't like the design of an instrument, and you assert, "It's the best design on the market," to him it may sound like, "Mr. Prospect, obviously you don't have enough knowledge or experience to recognize a better design when you see it!" Not exactly a way to have the prospect feeling good about you, your products and your company.

Don't Negate Your Prospect's Reality

When a prospect or customer responds with an objection to something you say, it is often based on personal experience or a perception of the issue. You can't tell the prospect that he's wrong or that it didn't happen. The customer's perception *is* his reality. You can't change that with just a quick response.

Even when a prospect steps outside his area of expertise and renders an opinion or feeling that may be incorrect, you must acknowledge it. It is irrelevant whether your prospect is a true expert or not. What matters is how he perceives himself and that you don't do or say anything that contradicts that perception or his experience.

How to Handle Objections in the Medical Sales Environment without Making the Medical Prospect Wrong: Go A.P.E. and C.

A. Acknowledge the objection. Medical professionals need to know that you hear what they are saying. Too many medical sales reps rush to answer an objection without really trying to understand the issue, the problem, or the circumstances that lead to the objection. There is also the possibility that you did not hear or interpret the objection properly. Acknowledging is the first step to ensure your proper understanding. There are several ways to acknowledge an objection. The simplest is to say, "Thank you. I'm glad you told me that." Notice that no point of contention is created and you did not agree with the objection. You merely acknowledged it.

Another way to acknowledge an objection is to repeat back or paraphrase what your prospect said in an empathetic way. For example, if your prospect says, "That device seems awfully complicated," you might reply, "I can certainly understand your impression that this device seems complicated."

Notice how this response puts you and the prospect on the same side, as opposed to positioning yourself opposite the prospect by responding, "It's not complicated!" You've created an area of agreement that does not place you in an adversarial position and allows the prospect to take a less defensive attitude. This paves the way for the next step, which is to get the prospect to elaborate his feelings and beliefs.

P. Probe the objection. Ask questions to probe deeper and verify if the objection is real. Remember that healthcare customers are averse to risks and may try to end a sales presentation quickly by throwing out superficial objections. You need to test objections by asking the prospect to explain each one.

Another benefit of asking questions is that it shows you are interested in the prospect's opinion. A professional medical sales rep would never ignore what the prospect is saying and just try to make his or her own point. Ask questions to show that you are focused on the interests of the prospect and her patients.

The purpose of the first probing question is to obtain information—not to disagree with the prospect or assert your opinion. Essentially, these questions say, "Tell me more." Ask more questions to have the prospect elaborate on his or her answers, if necessary.

You never know what you will learn when you question an objection. Anything the prospect tells you might be helpful to you in handling the objection and closing the sale. Information is power. Good questions get you good information.

E. **Explain to your prospect another point of view about the objection.** Responding to objections with healthcare professionals can be a delicate task. You want to avoid their perception of what you are saying as correcting them or trying to educate them. Again, they are the ones with the credentials and may resent these implications.

One way to explain a different point of view is to share the experiences and perceptions of your prospect's colleagues. Many sales professionals use a technique called *feel-felt-found*. It might sound something like this: "Ms. Adams, I understand how you *feel* about the weight of the device. Several of your colleagues *felt* the same way. Once they started using the device in their departments, they *found* that the increased speed of the device meant you didn't need to hold it as long, so the weight is not an issue." This serves to make the point without it seeming like it's coming from you.

Another way to explain or handle the objection, is to ask a "What if?" question. The "What if?" is useful if you can describe a scenario where your prospect's objection would be satisfied. If the prospect accepts the "What if?" as a solution and you can provide that solution, the objection is handled. An example is, "Ms. Adams, what if we could reduce the weight of the device by 50 percent. Would it fit within your specifications?" If your prospect agrees and you can deliver on the "What if?," the objection is handled.

C. Confirm that the objection is no longer a concern. It's a mistake to continue a presentation after responding to an objection without knowing whether or not your prospect accepts your explanation. First, it shows that you don't care enough about the prospect's feelings to hear his thoughts before continuing. Second, if the prospect is not satisfied with your response and you just continue, you are wasting your time and might be angering the prospect. Finally, if the prospect does not buy into your explanation, he may raise the same objection again later. Confirming the prospect's acceptance of your explanation immediately after it takes place is your opportunity to put the objection to rest for good.

Let's take a look at how the same sales conversation might go between Peter and Dr. Jones if Peter goes A.P.E.& C.

"Dr. Jones, what is your impression of the image quality?"

"Peter, I've got to tell you. I'm happy with the image quality on my old X-ray "machine. I don't see any advantages with your fancy, expensive digital machine."

"I can understand why you would feel that way. After all, your current X-ray equipment works fine doesn't it?"

"You bet it does. Plus it's paid for, and I don't need to mess with a computer to look at it. I just pop the film up on my view box."

"Is the need to use a computer one of your concerns about the digital system?"

"Peter, in any practice, time is money. I don't have the time to mess with a computer and I'll be retiring in about a year and selling my practice. I'm not about to learn how to use a fancy new digital system at this stage of my career."

What are the noticeable differences in this sales conversation? Notice how Peter avoided butting heads with Dr. Jones. Instead, he found some common ground by acknowledging that Dr. Jones's current X-ray machine works just fine.

At the same time, Peter's questions revealed some valuable information. Dr. Jones might be uncomfortable with the thought of using computer technology, but it seems like Peter identified a stronger reason—Dr. Jones is selling his practice in a year and does not want to invest in a new system and learn how to use it.

Peter is going to focus on Dr. Jones's desire to sell the practice. He's about to ask some questions to expose some problems associated with trying to sell a medical practice with antiquated X-ray equipment.

"If you're going to sell your practice, investing in a new digital imaging system may not intuitively seem like a good idea. Have you reviewed the current market for physician practices for sale and found out what is moving and what isn't?"

"No, but I have a solid practice and I'm sure that it will appeal to one of the new doctors coming into town. Besides, I'm willing to carry some of the debt, which will make it easier for a new doctor to buy the practice."

"Dr. Jones, a recent study in Family Practice Economics showed that practices sold most quickly when offered as a turnkey operation, with modern, state-of-the-art equipment. Are you going to offer your practice as a turnkey operation?"

"Absolutely. Everything is included."

"Dr. Jones, that same article in Family Practice Economics said that 89 percent of the residents and fellows in the United States have some training with digital imaging. For many, it's the standard of care. How will you handle that issue?"

"Well, if they want digital X-ray, they are going to have to buy it on their own."

"So if I understand you correctly, you are willing to reduce the asking price of your practice to compensate for the investment that the new practitioner will need to make to bring it up to his or her standards?"

"I won't need to reduce the price. If someone wants the practice, they'll pay what I'm asking!"

"You've been in practice for a long time, and no doubt, your practice has a lot of value. Let me ask you something. If you were a new doctor shopping for a practice in this town, and it came down to buying one of two practices, with all things being equal including price, which practice would you buy—one with an imaging system that you consider to be outdated, or one with a modern digital system that you're used to?"

"I see your point, Peter. But financially, it doesn't make sense for me. I will only be able to take one year's depreciation on the cost of a new system if I sell the practice in a year. Why should I pay up front on an expensive system to hand over the tax benefits to the doctor who buys my practice?"

"Dr. Jones, I understand your feelings completely. On one hand, it doesn't make sense to make a large investment in something that will only benefit you and your practice for one year. But on the other hand, we both know that modernizing the most important piece of equipment in your practice is going to make your practice sellable at top dollar. Dr. Jones, *what if* I can show you a way that you can accelerate the depreciation on the new equipment in the first year such that you get 80 percent of the total tax benefit and your net investment would be minimal? Would it be worth continuing our discussion?"

"Yes, it would. But I'm still not enthralled with computers . . . "

"Computers can be a bit intimidating at first. Do you think you would be comfortable touching a patient's name on a screen with your finger and touching a box that says "view image?"

"That doesn't sound too hard."

"That's all you need to do. So you think you can get comfortable using digital equipment."

"It seems simple enough. Show me how this thing works . . . "

A.P.E. & C. is an effective way to handle objections in the medical environment. Of course, it must be used in a natural way appropriate to the situation. If you don't do anything else before responding to an objection, at least acknowledge it. It shows that you are empathetic to the professional's feelings and not just a salesman out for his or her own good. Using questions to clarify or verify an objection is also a good idea to make sure you fully understand your prospect's concerns. You'll discover whether the objection is real or not, which is important, because objections that don't really matter are a big waste of time.

Emotional Objections

While many objections are based on your prospect's perception or misperception of your product or service, other objections may have an emotional basis. When you consider the stressful environment of healthcare, your customers' high expectations of you and your company to provide good service, and the customer's ego, it's easy to see why emotional objections occur.

Objections may be the offspring of any of the following emotions:

• Anger

- Fear
- Resentment
- Embarrassment
- Frustration
- Lack of trust
- Impatience

Anger is an emotion that can short-circuit rational thinking. Imagine a prospect who is angered over an event that occurred earlier in the day, maybe right before seeing you. Such an emotion may place him in a cynical state of mind. On more than one occasion, I attempted a sales conversation with a customer who seemed angry over something, with them finding nothing but fault with anything I said. Days or weeks later, after the customer had a chance to cool off, he or she would respond in a very different, more rational way.

Some customers might be harboring anger from years earlier. There was one surgeon in my territory, Dr. Say, who would never grant me an appointment to meet with him in his office. Whenever I saw him in the hospital and attempted to speak with him, he always had a negative, nasty attitude. After a year of dealing with his behavior, I finally summoned the courage to ask why he always seemed angry whenever I tried to show him one of my products. Dr. Say got red in the face, leaned forward and said, "When I came to town eight years ago, I never saw a rep from your company. I trained on all of your company's products when I was in residency, and your company didn't have the decency to have a rep call on me. So, you come along seven years later and want my business. You can forget it—it's too late." I could see the anger in his eyes. It is difficult to have a rational conversation with an angry customer until you deal with the anger first.

Fear is an emotion that healthcare providers may experience relative to trying new products. Imagine a clinician who treated a patient using a product or service similar to yours, but with less than satisfactory results. He may fear the incident will repeat itself if he tries your product. And if the results are not good, your customer fears getting sued and fears his or her reputation could be compromised.

Resentment can have several causes, but I have seen it occur most commonly when one customer feels that another customer is getting more attention, better service, better pricing or opportunities to use new products first. A customer may truly resent it if he or she believes that a fellow healthcare provider or institution gets preferential treatment from your company. It doesn't matter as to whether or not *you* believe those feelings are justified. Again, the customer's perception is the customer's reality.

I had one surgeon who used one or two of my products each month, who suggested that I took better care of some of the other surgeons in the hospital. It took me a while to uncover where this feeling came from, but one time, when I asked him why he wouldn't use more of my products, he said, "Because Dr. Petersen always gets to use your stuff first. When you're ready to let me be first, then we'll talk." This surgeon resented my allowing Dr. Petersen to use my products before him. Realistically, because Dr. Petersen was a much busier surgeon, he always had more opportunities to use what I sold.

If a customer resents you or your actions, talking about how your product will make his life easier, help his patients, etc., is a waste of time. You must first uncover the source of resentment and deal with it, or no business will occur.

Another thing that causes resentment is when a salesperson tries to educate healthcare experts that don't want to be educated by a salesperson. As I discussed previously, doctors and other professionals see themselves as the authority, and some resent it when a salesperson tries to teach them what they already know (or should know). Careful communication, in a way that it does not seem like you are telling the customer how to practice medicine, can help prevent this.

Embarrassment is an emotion that can cause a prospect to retreat from you and your product. Imagine that your presentation uncovers some information that the prospect doesn't know, but as a professional, should know. The prospect may try to hide his or her embarrassment by attempting to find fault with your product. If you can find a way to take ownership of the situation in a way that allows the prospect to save face, you might be able to recover the sale.

I had one hospital buyer who told her administrator she was getting the best price possible from my company. She was getting a good price, but truthfully, we never discussed it. The hospital administrator found out that a hospital in a neighboring county was getting a better price, and when he confronted the buyer, she was embarrassed. The buyer became angry with me! The other hospital wasn't in my territory and I had no knowledge of the pricing. But the buyer felt embarrassed in front of her administrator for not getting the best price, and so she felt the only way she could save face was to buy from another company. The buyer tried to cover this up with fabricated objections, but after continued probing, she eventually told me the truth. Fortunately, I found a way for her to save face and for me to save the business. I was able to bundle some products together in a package that reduced the customer's overall expense and made the buyer look like a hero. It also locked in the business with my company for the subsequent two years!

Frustration is another emotion that hails from many different sources in the medical environment. Perhaps your prospect is frustrated after reviewing several products similar to yours and still not finding exactly what he is looking for. He might have some pre-conceived notion as to what a particular product or service should look like. When he doesn't find it, he feels frustrated. One way for the customer to end the frustration is to end the sales conversation, possibly by bombarding you with objections.

Lack of trust by the customer is a fatal blow, not only to your presentation, but to any future business with that customer. If your customer does not trust you, he or she will offer up every reason in the world not to use your product. A trust issue may not have anything to do with you personally, but may stem from a previous experience with your company or the previous sales representative that you replaced. Identifying and solving a lack-of-trust issue is mission-critical if you ever plan to have that prospect as a customer. Remember, their patients trust them with their lives. Your customers need to trust that you and your products will do what they expect.

Impatience is frequently a character trait of medical professionals. It is bred by an urgent desire to solve problems *now*. If a customer believes that learning how to use your product will take too long or that it will prolong the treatment process, they may decline. Patients expect fast results and healthcare providers feel a pressure to deliver. If your product or service takes longer to use or longer to learn, you can anticipate some impatience.

If you really want to see healthcare professionals become impatient, deliver sales presentations that drag on and on. Often, they just want you to get to the point, so they can make a decision. But sometimes, their impatience is nothing more than an effort to end your sales presentation. Stay focused on problems and solutions, and don't over-elaborate.

Handling the Emotional Objection

Whenever you detect or suspect an emotional objection, you need to stop focusing on the product and instead, focus on the emotional issue. It makes little sense to give a sales presentation to someone that has negative feelings about you, your product, or your company.

The best way to neutralize an emotional objection is to give the customer an opportunity to express his or her feelings, acknowledge those feelings and then apologize, if appropriate. Often, the customer just wants to know that someone from your company cares about something that occurred. You can be this person by showing empathy with a statement such as, "That must have been very upsetting," or "I can understand why you feel the way that you do." Show that you understand the customer's feelings and give them an opportunity to fully express them. It helps to disarm any negative emotions since it is difficult to express those emotions with someone who is sympathetic to your way of thinking.

An apology can be an effective way to get the customer to put the issue to rest. Before issuing an apology, I must caution you to be sure that you are not apologizing for an issue that could have legal implications since such an apology may be used against you or your company as an admission of guilt. If you're not sure whether an apology is appropriate or not, it's a good idea to seek counsel from management in your company.

You can express regret for an event that occurred, even though you were not the offending party. Just a simple, "I'm sorry that happened to you" can go a long way to soothe an upset customer along with your assurances that it will never happen again or happen with you.

When you are dealing with an event for which you are personally responsible, and there is no risk of legal liability, a heartfelt apology will often resolve the issue quickly. The apology must be delivered with sincerity.

I had an operating room director who was very upset with my company for several years. She discovered that Henry, the sales representative before me, billed the hospital for products he never delivered. It didn't feel right apologizing for Henry's behavior, because I had no control over it and had never even met him. I said, "I understand your anger over what Henry did. I am sorry that he left you with a bad impression about my company. I want to fix that. Tell me what I can do?"

I *was* sorry that Henry gave my company a bad name, but I did not apologize to accept responsibility for his actions. I wanted to show that I cared. The customer opened up and shared with me other reasons for not doing business with my company over the years. She also told me exactly what I needed to do to earn back her trust, and that was very valuable information. I did what she asked and over time, I regained her trust and the business.

Make Sure You Never Respond to an Objection Emotionally

Your prospects and customers may occasionally hit you with objections and statements that get your dander up. For example, a customer may anger you by saying something about you personally such as, "I don't think you know your product as well as you should." Or perhaps your emotions are building because you're frustrated by a lack of progress during your presentation. Maybe you feel embarrassed because you said something that wasn't correct and your customer chided you for it. Learn to recognize your own emotions, and don't speak or act as a result of those emotions.

Never respond emotionally during a conversation with a customer;

you might say something you will regret. The best medical sales professionals know how to pause, take a deep breath and think before speaking, so they can respond directly to the situation or problem and not to their own emotions.

All of the research on the subject of emotional intelligence has demonstrated one simple fact:

When Emotions Go Up, Intelligence Goes Down

To prove this point, consider how many times you or someone that you know said something foolish during a heated conversation. Later, you thought, "I wish I hadn't said that!" When people are experiencing extremes of emotion—including euphoria—they may say things they don't really mean. Sometimes, even stupid things come out of people's mouths because they cannot think of anything appropriate at the moment. How many times after an emotional encounter have you said, "I wish I had said this or that?" Once your emotions cool down, you are able to think intelligently again, and you think of the things you wish you had said. Understand that any time you're feeling anger, euphoria or any other strong emotions, your mind might not be working at its best.

Preventing your own emotional response is another reason to acknowledge all objections. The time that it takes to acknowledge the objection and get feedback from your prospect provides the necessary time than is needed to formulate an intelligent response, as opposed to an emotional one. Learn to take time with your responses. Remember—the first response to an objection that pops into your head may not be the best one—especially if you are responding out of emotion.

Dealing with Objections Based on Scientific Studies

Objections based on published scientific studies may sometimes seem impossible to handle, but it's doable. Preparation is the key, along with the ability to effectively probe how the scientific data affects the buying decision in your prospect's mind.

Many professionals in the medical world are well versed in academic literature and may raise objections based on factual evidence that was obtained through legitimate research. Adequate preparation on your part requires that you familiarize yourself with any and all scientific papers that relate to your product or service. This helps you to anticipate factual objections and to formulate a plan to handle them.

A simple way to prepare is to use the Internet to get a list of the most recent papers relating to your product or service. There are sites online that have access to free articles, but you may need to use paid services, as well. Pay attention to the journals and websites that target your segment of the healthcare industry. Anything that is published may affect your customers' thinking.

If you are getting repeated objections based on articles or other academic research, then you need to learn how to dissect this information with someone from your company or a knowledgeable medical professional who can help you plan your rebuttal. Scientific studies can sometimes be interpreted to mean different things. Your competitors may be offering up a study with a completely different interpretation from what you might present. The key is in knowing how to highlight the information that conveys the information that benefits your argument.

Scientific studies sometimes involve protocols and patient populations that limit the scope and validity of the data. Knowing how to expose these limitations to suggest that the results of the study may not be 100 percent accurate can be useful, especially when combating your competitors' use of the same study. Again, if you don't make time to research and familiarize yourself with all of the pertinent literature, you'll find yourself pinned against the wall by a customer or competitor who knows more than you do.

When a customer is quoting scientific literature, he may just be parroting what he heard from a colleague or one of your competitors. He may have never actually read the scientific study he is referencing. Your ability to confidently discuss a scientific paper and interpret its outcome will help insure that your prospects have the right information, but be careful not to embarrass the prospect when discussing any differences between what they stated and what is actually presented in the paper.

Reframing Challenges Dealing with Factual Objections

Some objections can't be disputed, due to the fact that they are, well, facts. If "It is what it is," and you can't change the facts, you need to change the way the customer considers those facts. For example, instead of the customer focusing on one or two reason not to buy, reframe the presentation so that the customer sees how your product or service will help him to achieve his overall goal, despite any perceived reasons not to move forward.

In the last example, where Paul is trying to get Dr. Jones to consider purchasing a digital X-ray, the customer's real objection was that he could not see the value of investing a large amount of money into his practice when he would be retiring and selling it in a year. How did Paul reframe Dr. Jones's objection?

Retirement means that Dr. Jones's needs to sell his practice, and this is most likely an important goal. Instead of allowing Dr. Jones to focus on what seemed like a waste of money because he was retiring, Paul reframed the digital X-ray machine as a key feature of Dr. Jones's practice that would ultimately influence a potential buyer.

You might not be able to make a factual objection go away, but you can often minimize it in terms of the overall big picture. The ultimate, altruistic goal of every healthcare provider and institution is to serve the patient's needs. Demonstrate how your product or service can do that, and many objections shrink in significance.

Take the "cost" objection (e.g., "Your product or service costs too much."). The most common method of dealing with a cost objection is to present a cost justification. This is essentially a reframing technique, in which you get the customer to focus on how the cost of your product or service is less than the overall cost of what they are doing now, or how failing to get your product will cost more over time, all things considered.

Remember, the best way to educate your "expert" customers is through the use of questions to get *them to tell you* what is best for them, their institutions, and their patients. Ask questions that get your prospects to focus on their ultimate goals and many factual objections will become irrelevant.

Objections—Why Not Avoid Them in the First Place?

By now, you should be convinced that objections are mainly a good thing that help move the sales process forward. But too many objections may hinder your efforts by creating a negative overall impression for your prospect. Some objections can be prevented, and when this is possible, it makes little sense not to do so. So, how do you prevent objections?

Over time, you will discover certain objections that seem to come up on a regular basis for each product or service. If you are getting the same objection more than 50 percent of time, why wait for the prospect to raise the objection? Handle it before it even comes up; work it into your data presentation. For example, if you routinely hear that a medical instrument feels heavy and you normally respond to the objection by telling the prospect that the instrument does not weigh more, but is balanced differently; include this information in your presentation. You might say, "Some of the clinicians who have used this instrument commented that it seems heavier than similar instruments, but it actually weighs about same as the other instruments on the market, and the heavier feeling is due to the way that the instrument is balanced, which creates less hand fatigue for the user." Notice that the objection was mentioned in the presentation, along with the response, which not only explains the weight issue, but demonstrates it as a benefit.

Don't make it a goal to respond to every objection preemptively, just the ones that seem to come up over and over. If you overdo it, you will be helping your prospect find fault with your product and create objections. When you can reduce the number of objections by eliminating the common ones, your prospect may be left with a better gut feeling about your product or service, because he or she has expressed fewer reasons not to buy.

Maintain an Objection Log

Debriefing after every presentation helps to avoid repeating what didn't work and helps you to continue to do what did. When you hear new objections, record them in an objection log during your debrief.

It's a sad thing when a salesperson hears the same objection over and over, yet can't remember how to handle it. This often results from a failure to review the objections for a given product and the appropriate explanation to handle the objection.

Keep a list of every objection for each product or service you sell. If you're just starting out and your company has not provided you with such a list, start to construct one on your own by asking other salespeople, managers and product managers what objections they have heard regarding the product or service.

After listing the objections, record a list of all the possible responses you can come up with. Brainstorm on your own and with your fellow sales professionals, so you know exactly how to respond to each objection, should it arise. Plan your A.P.E. strategy ahead of time, as well. How will you acknowledge each objection? What questions will you ask to probe and verify the validity of the objection? And finally, have as many responses as possible that will neutralize, or at least minimize, the objection.

Preparation is the Number One Key to Handling Objections

The most common fear about objections in medical sales is that the salesperson won't be able to handle them. Because your customers are experts in their respective specialties, you need to be prepared for any objections they might throw at you. Start an objection log by listing every objection that you and your sales colleagues can think of. Brainstorm the entire A.P.E. approach. Study it and practice it. When you hear new objections, add them to your repertoire. If a particular approach to handling an objection is effective, keep it; if not, scrap it.

Develop an absolute belief that you can handle objections. Welcome objections when they show up, because your customer won't buy until and unless you can neutralize or eliminate the objections. Be *grateful* for every new one you discover.

Objections not only keep the sales process alive, they help move it towards completion. When you use the A.P.E. and C. approach to handle objections, you are allowing the customer to help you build the case to buy your product or service. Once objections are out of the way, your goal is to get the customer to commit to the next sensible step. That is the subject of the next chapter.

Presentation Skills: Closing

Do you know the difference between a good sales call and a visit?

In selling, it is very easy to become trapped in the idea that any time we spend in the company of a prospect or customer is productive. This may be true on some levels, but from purely a sales perspective, it is not. Too many medical sales representatives categorize a sales call as good whenever they get to spend a few minutes with the prospect and don't get thrown out of the office.

Here is what I believe to be true—a sales call is good only if it results in a sale or advances the sale by getting a commitment from the prospect or customer to take the next step.

Closing is getting your prospect to commit to the logical next step that advances or completes the sale.

You're Closing All the Time

By focusing on the prospect's needs and desires and demonstrating how you can fulfill them, you are closing the sale during each step. Getting a prospect to say "Yes," to your product or service is nothing more than the sum total of "Yeses," that you get throughout the presentation.

The Simple Truth about Closing—
Someone Has To Do It

Closing can occur in two ways:

The prospect says, "I'll take it," on his own, asks to evaluate the product or service or asks to take the next step to advance the sale.

or

The salesperson asks the prospect to buy, evaluate or commit to the next step of the sale.

If neither No. 1 nor No. 2 occurs, then the sales presentation is dead in the water. While it might seem unfathomable to allow the sales process to come skidding to a halt after all of the preceding effort, it happens all the time. I have witnessed countless sales presentations where the business was neither offered nor asked for.

Jim is one of the best presenters in medical device sales. He knows how to gracefully open a presentation, ask probing questions that uncover pain and problems, deliver a complex and technical sales presentation in such a way that the features and benefits of his products are crystal clear, and he can handle objections like a consummate professional. Jim's one flaw is that he won't ask for the business.

Why do so many sales professionals have such difficulty asking for the business? If you ask them, most will tell you that they don't want to act like a used car salesman and be perceived as pushy. Some will tell you that they don't even want to be perceived as salespeople at all, but as consultants.

Do you think there is any question in your prospect's mind about what you do for a living? I assure you that when you walk into a prospect's office, hospital, clinic or other facility and have a conversation about how your products can solve their problems, they know you are in sales! You can call yourself a consultant, a technical advisor or anything else you can think of, but you won't be paid unless you sell something. Your prospects know this, and they *expect* you to ask for the business.

There will be times when your prospects will recognize the value of your offering and tell you that they want your product or service without you ever asking. But don't wait for this to happen—it is your job to ask for the business and the prospect expects it.

Closing is Easy . . . When Everything Else Is Done Correctly

As you have gone through your presentation, asking the right questions and competently handling objections, your prospect has helped build the case to support using your product or service. Having verified numerous points of agreement supporting the ways your product can solve the clinician's problem or improve the patient's outcome, asking for the business should be comfortable and easy.

But, what happens when your prospect does little more than find fault with your product or service and reasons not to use them? Asking for the business feels awkward if the prospect doesn't agree with any of your presented benefits.

Even when it's awkward, your job is to ask for the business. You need to focus on one or more reasons to buy, despite your prospect's objections (reframing). Use stories to support the way other healthcare professionals and their patients benefited from your product and then ask for some commitment to move the sale forward—even if you don't feel like it! What is the worst that can happen? They will say "No." At least you will know you have done your job and asked for the business.

Expect the Sale—Assume the Sale

The *Law of Expectations* plays a big part in your success as a medical sales professional. *Assume the sale* at every sales opportunity. If you approach the close with doubt or the expectation that the prospect probably won't buy, you will usually get what you expect.

A salesperson's expectations are often palpable when he or she is discussing a product. If you lack enthusiasm, confidence and an assumptive attitude regarding your ability to close the sale, it probably won't happen. Use assumptive language such as, "When you start using the new device," as opposed to "If you use the new device."

You represent a good product or service, right? Then expect your customers to want it! After all, why would you waste your time and your prospects' time discussing a product or service that you don't believe they will buy? When you truly believe that your product will improve your customer's ability to care for his or her patients, asking for the business is easier, because you expect to hear a *"Yes!"* Every time you discuss your product with anyone, tell yourself, "She is going to love this product! She is going to want it for her patients!" Make sure that *you* believe it.

Closing Doesn't Have To Be Fancy

Many types of sales focus on the salesperson's ability to close (e.g., the automobile industry). Some sales training programs stress the need to rattle off 25 closing techniques in succession until the prospect says yes. While some of these closing approaches might work in other industries, launching a closing "attack" in the medical world could ruin your career.

Medical professionals are intelligent buyers who like to make decisions based on facts—not pressure or prefabricated sales closes. Even when you are addressing emotional issues that relate to your product or service, you will frequently use a factual approach. When the sum of the facts supports a reason to buy, all you need to do is ask for the business.

It's often helpful to begin with a brief summary of the reasons why the prospect should buy. Summarize what you have already discussed: the problem, the consequences of ignoring the problem and the agreed-upon benefits of solving the problem. It might go something like this:

"Doctor, we have discussed the potential problem of an electrosurgical pad that does not adhere to the skin and how that can cause a severe burn to the patient. We talked about how ignoring this problem could lead to a courtroom. You commented about how the monitoring system on our new electrosurgical unit can prevent patients from ever suffering a burn. Can I get you to sign off on a letter stating that you support evaluating the new pad?"

A good close is time-related to create immediacy. For example, if you are selling a device or product that is used on a patient-by-patient basis, you could ask, "Do you have any procedures during the next two weeks where you can evaluate the device?" If the prospect answers, "Yes," you can simply ask, "Can we take a look at your schedule to choose which procedure you would like to use it on, so I can have [the product or service] available for you?"

Notice that in the above example, you did not just ask, "Are you willing to try it?" This leaves an infinite time frame for the prospect to decide. The response that you will usually get in this situation is, "I'll keep it in mind and call you when I need it." The prospect might remember to call you, but in the busy medical environment, it is likely that the prospect will continue to use whatever he is using and forget about you and your offering. This is why it is important to try and nail the prospect down to a specific opportunity on a specific date.

There are many ways that you can phrase the closing question. Another variation might be, "Doctor, can we take a look at your schedule for the next 30 days and find one or two cases for you to try it out?"

There are almost infinite ways to ask for the business—the important thing is that you get a definite commitment.

What if you are selling a product that needs to be approved by a product evaluation committee before it will be allowed into the hospital? Your closing question might be, "Who should I speak with on the product committee to get the ball rolling about starting an evaluation?"

Again, always expect to hear a "Yes," when you ask for a commitment. An assumptive attitude projects confidence that makes it easier for the prospect to say "Yes."

Speaking of "Yes," once the sale is made—stop selling. For some reason, there are sales people who feel the need to reinforce the prospect's decision to move forward even after the prospect has given the go-ahead. Your prospect could find your continued sales efforts annoying. Even worse, you could bring something up that the prospect had not considered which could squash the sale. Once the prospect says, "Let's give it a try" or "Write up the order," *stop selling!* The only thing you should be focused on now is processing the sale and delivering your product or service in a timely and competent manner.

How should you handle it when the prospect says "No?" Don't pack up your stuff and start heading for the door just yet. Too many sales people accept defeat too easily, tuck their tails between their legs and leave. This is a huge mistake.

As a medical sales professional, be prepared to ask for the business multiple times. Expect to hear a few "Nos" from a prospect before hearing a "Yes." Treat a "No" response as the prospect's way of telling you that he doesn't have enough reasons to say "Yes" yet. Find out why the prospect doesn't feel that your product or service is a good fit. How do you do this? Go A.P.E (see chapter 14).

Handle a "No" the same as you would handle an objection, because any reason for not buying *is* an objection. When you get a "No," acknowledge the fact that the customer is not ready to buy. You could say, "I'm sorry, Peggy. Based on our conversation, I thought that you were ready to move ahead. I understand that you are not ready."

Find out why the prospect is not buying by asking. "Peggy, just so I'm clear ... help me to understand why you do not wish to move forward at this time?" If you're not comfortable with that approach because it makes you feel too pushy, then blame the question on someone else: "Peggy, could you help me out with something? I will be speaking with my manager about our appointment today and he is going to want to know why you are not moving forward with our product. Help me out—what should I tell him?" Some sales reps are more comfortable asking the question this way, because they are shifting the focus of the need to know onto someone else.

Once you know why the prospect isn't buying, try to handle the objection. Make an attempt to address the prospect's concerns and ask for the business again: "Peggy, now that we have moved that problem out of the way, should I speak with someone on the product evaluation committee so we can get the ball rolling?"

Sometimes, the prospect may ask for information that you will need to gather. Immediately schedule a time to provide the requested information. Don't work with a nebulous time frame, such as, "I'll call you in a few weeks." If you don't set a solid appointment for follow-up, your efforts to do so may be difficult and frustrating. When your prospect is seriously considering doing business with you, he or she will give you a follow-up appointment.

Beware of the prospect who requests additional information as a stalling tactic. You can test her sincerity by using a trial close. You might say, "Peggy, I will get you the information you are requesting by next Tuesday at 1 p.m. If you find that the product specifications meet your criteria, what else needs to take place in order for us to move forward?"

If the prospect shows a willingness to continue the sales process, you know that it is worth the effort to do what she asks. You have also set a level of expectation. However, if she replies by telling you, "There won't be any money for this available until next year," then you know where you stand. Unless you can find a way to circumvent the current budget issue, you need to place this sale in the queue for next year and move on to more immediate opportunities.

Always assume the sale, but always verify that your assumptions are correct.

In Medical Sales, Closing Can Take Time

Because medical professionals make buying decisions that affect the well-being of their patients and their own professional future, many like to take their time before committing. Especially when considering new products that are not yet supported by long-term research and follow-up, some customers might say, "It looks good. Let's talk again when you have more published data and I'll consider it at that time."

Do not make the mistake of abandoning an opportunity because you can't close it today. Just as medical sales involves building long-term relationships and a commitment to providing service, it also requires keeping your customers updated throughout a product's cycle and determining when they are ready to buy. Repeated sales calls and conversations about a product or service are often the key to getting your prospect to give your product or service serious consideration. In time, as you share the positive experiences of other customers, the prospect might be ready to give your product a try.

Whenever there are any product updates or published literature that support the efficacy and good patient outcomes of your product or service, make sure to inform your prospects and customers. Ask for the business again, again and again until the prospect says "Yes," or informs you that he has no intention of ever using that product and doesn't want to discuss it anymore. But, unless you get that kind of true rejection, don't give up.

Show That You Have Class

Whether you get the sale or not, send a nice, handwritten thank-you note to your prospects and customers to thank them for their time and interest. It only takes a minute or two and it distinguishes you from your competitors. In fact, you should think of this step as part of the close. I can assure you, few medical sales professionals take the time to send a handwritten thank-you note. Make sure you write it on quality stationery and not a preprinted mini-ad for your business. These notes are especially important when you are new in your territory, but it will get you a lot of mileage with your customers throughout your career. A thank-you note demonstrates that you appreciate and value the prospect's time, shows that you are detail-oriented (which is critically important in medical sales) and that you have class. If you're serious about succeeding in this field, get serious about sending thank-you notes.

You Must Close To Succeed In Medical Sales

A sales call is successful *only* if it results in:

- The order, (i.e., buying the product or scheduling an evaluation)
- Advancing the sale, (i.e. getting a commitment to move to the next step of the sales process, for example, attending a professional course)

A sales call is not successful if all you have done is spend time to build rapport—that's a courtesy call or a professional visit. Building rapport is important, but it won't pay your mortgage or put food on your family's table.

Don't be a professional visitor. Close for commitment on every call!

16

Account Penetration Strategies
Working the Hospital

Selling in hospitals can be an intimidating experience if you don't know the terrain, and even sometimes when you do. Hospitals are not just centers of patient care—they are huge corporations that operate in many ways like other large businesses. Effectively working the hospital requires the medical sales professional to approach it not only from a patient care perspective, but also with an understanding of the hospital's need to operate and succeed as a business.

A daunting task for sales reps new to hospital selling is sorting through the layers of personnel who are involved with product or service selection and utilization. The medical sales professional must create and maintain relationships with any and all hospital employees involved in the decision process for his products or services. In addition, he or she has to effectively sell based on each staff member's unique interests and needs.

There may be several call points for your products or services that require you to interact with personnel from any of the following departments:

Hospital administration   Pharmacy
Hospital staff physicians   Nursing/Medical Education
Nursing Services   Anesthesia
Intensive Care Units   Biomedical Engineering
Operating Room   Environmental Services
Materials management   Risk Management
Infection Control   Radiology
Product Evaluation Committee   Laboratory/Pathology
Central/Sterile Processing   Rehabilitation Services

If you're new to medical sales, you might be wondering how all those other departments garner a say in what products and services get used, when it seems like a clinical decision. You must know the call points for your product and make sure you don't ignore any key personnel, or you could end up losing the sale.

Let's assume that you sell a vascular catheter that is used to monitor central venous pressure in patients. As you might guess, a doctor would order the placement of this catheter. Most likely a surgeon or anesthesiologist would insert the catheter into the patient. Seeing as doctors decide what type of catheter to use, how do the other departments come into play?

Some of the other departments have a vested interest in the product that is used. Let's take radiology, for example. Because these catheters are placed in critically ill patients, there is a good chance that such a patient might require imaging with an MRI at some point during their treatment. There are a few considerations for any implantable items with respect to MRI.

The first consideration is whether or not the catheter contains any materials that can interfere with the MRI image. Certain metals can cause what is called "scatter" in the image, making it unreadable. Perhaps this interference could be bypassed by using a different diagnostic modality, such as CT imaging. Also, any ferrous materials can be displaced or even ripped out of the body by the powerful magnetic field of the MRI. This is truly a life and death consideration.

It is also important to know if and to what extent the catheter is radiopaque or radiolucent, that is, the product's ability to be seen on X-ray to verify position, but also to allow visualization of any structures behind it. These are all important considerations.

That's just one example of how a department such as radiology has a vested interest in the way another department, such as the operating room, selects products. What about some of the other departments mentioned?

Infection Control could have an interest, because the catheter provides a track from outside the body to the inside. Does this significantly increase the risk of infection and if so, how might that risk be managed?

Would *nursing services* need to change protocols or equipment to use the new catheter? Would it require a significant investment of time and money in retraining staff?

If the catheter interfaces with any other equipment, such as a monitor, does it create any compatibility issues or meet the safety requirements for the *Biomedical Engineer*?

If any medications that might be delivered via the catheter need to be in a form other than what is currently used, does the *Pharmacy Department* needs to be consulted?

Materials Management is concerned regarding the ordering, stocking and delivery of the catheters to the departments where it will be used. What are the overall costs of obtaining the catheter and would it affect any existing buying contracts already in place?

The list could go on and on. That is why hospitals have created product evaluation committees to review products that are being considered for use in the facility. It is also why your sales approach includes not just the end-users, but all concerned parties.

Product Evaluation Committees

Think about a general election. The people choose who gets elected by each person casting a vote. Does each voter make his or her choice according to how they think a candidate will serve *all* of the constituents? Some might, but most voters choose a candidate they believe will best serve the voter's own interests, the voter's own WIIFM!

Product committees are similar to a population electing a candidate or voting on an issue. Each committee member needs to choose products or services based on many factors. The reasons they vote to approve a purchase, put it on hold or deny it might be very different than what you would expect. You need to uncover and address each committee member's specific concerns, whether it's a committee of one or a committee of 20.

Almost all hospitals have some type of product evaluation committee, also known as a product review committee. The purpose of the product evaluation committee is to make certain that all interests are represented in the product decision-making process. These committees include representatives from many departments beyond traditional clinical positions and product end-users, including hospital administrators, infection control practitioners, risk managers and purchasing personnel.

The committee approach to product selection ensures that all departments and key personnel have a say. Safety, cost and standardization are the issues most commonly addressed.

The key to successfully working with product evaluation committees is to identify the main concerns for each member. Considering that some committees may have upwards of a dozen members, this may seem like a daunting task. It requires some work, but if you take a systematic approach, it is not as difficult as it may seem.

Product evaluation committees can delay the time it takes to get your product into the hands of the end user. Some facilities have very strict policies that restrict any product from clinical use prior to being approved by the committee. However, in some institutions, you might be able to get an exemption or temporary approval for your product prior to it being reviewed by the committee. The end-user may need to plead his case to get temporary approval from the hospital. Sometimes, this is done on a case-by-case basis until the product receives formal approval or denial from the committee.

Committees meet at regular intervals, usually once a month, depending on the institution. Your product may not get on the agenda for several months. When your product is reviewed, some committees will approve or deny products at the committee meeting. Others will require a review of the minutes by all members with a formal submission of each member's decision. This can delay the final decision by weeks or even months in the event that the product needs to be scheduled on the agenda for final review.

Make sure you have an understanding of this process at the beginning, so you understand the timeline and plan accordingly.

Build Relationships

While everyone knows how important it is to build long-term relationships with a product's and service's end-user, it is equally important to build similar relationships with members of the product evaluation committee. Interaction with committee members may be ongoing with respect to current products and services, as well as products or services that you would like to sell in the future.

Find Your Champion and Your Coach

Selling to product evaluation committees can be a challenge, especially in terms of having access to the key personnel. Because many of these people are busy professionals, they don't always take time to meet with salespeople unless someone in a key position in the buying process asks them to.

It will benefit you to find someone to *champion* your cause and someone to *coach* you through the buying process. Your champion and coach can be the same person or different people, depending on what they know, who they know and whether or not they are willing to be an advocate on your behalf.

When seeking a champion, consider any clinicians or hospital employees who see benefits in your product or service for themselves, the hospital and the patients.

Physicians, department managers or supervisors are good candidates, especially when they have some level of influence. Ideally, you need someone who will solicit support from other users and potential users of your product or service and lobby members of the product committee on your behalf.

A healthcare professional or hospital employee might choose to be a champion if your product does any of the following:

- Creates better patient outcomes
- Reduces risk
- Saves cost

- Saves time for provider
- Reduces length of hospital stay
- Elevates the public's perception of the provider and the institution
- Reduces pain
- Reduces complications
- Increases reimbursement

Keep in mind that your champion may not be a strong salesperson. It will be very helpful if your champion is open to allowing you to *coach* him or her on how to sell your product or service to the product evaluation committee. In other words, you provide them with the ammo and they do the shooting!

Take your champions through the same selling steps that we discussed in this book. They must be able to discuss some problem or pain that your product or service can solve. Provide a list of questions that will help your champion to get members of the committee to focus on the problem and pain. Discuss with your champion how to stir the pain by discussing the implications of continuing to do without your product or service. Prepare your champion with a list of anticipated objections he or she may receive from committee members and how to handle them. Finally, help your champions to ask for the business by tying your product or service into benefits for the hospital, themselves and the patient.

What If You Can't Find A Champion?

If you can't find a champion, then you will need to connect with members of the product evaluation committee on your own. It's a good idea to do this even when you have a champion, because you are in the best position to educate them about the benefits of your product, even though you don't have the same level of influence as one of their colleagues.

I suggest you find a coach, someone in the hospital or clinic to coach you on how to connect with the right people on the product evaluation committee. Your coach can also direct you to other personnel that can provide you with information to strengthen the case for your product or service.

Consider personnel with whom you have good relationships and a solid history of providing good service. Customers who like you will generally try to help you if you ask them to and it doesn't violate their fiduciary duty to their employer. Essentially, you're asking them to point you in the right direction, give you helpful advice regarding members of the committee and to help you get some face time with these people.

Sometimes, salespeople are invited to the product committee meetings, but more often they are not, so information is going to be presented about your product and you might not be there to clarify or defend it. Even if you are permitted to attend the meeting, you might not be able to address every individual concern. It is better to try and speak with each member in advance.

Decide which people on the product committee are most important for you to contact. Your champion or coach could help you with this. Contact the appropriate committee members and request a brief meeting to address specific concerns this person may have about your product or service. Your goal is to talk to each person about his or her main issues with respect to your product. Don't give the same presentation that you give to clinicians unless it is appropriate and relevant. Find out where the potential problems or concerns are for each person and know how you can address it. Make sure you are answering each person's WIIFM question.

Your champion, coach, and other hospital staff should be familiar with many of the product committee members' concerns. Again, you must be fully prepared to meet with any committee member.

Schedule a Meeting with the Committee Member

Would you like a way to get committee members to take your call and schedule a meeting? The easiest way to do this is to be referred by another manager, supervisor, hospital executive or clinician. Busy healthcare executives and professionals won't normally meet with a salesperson unless a relationship is already established. The exception is when the salesperson is referred by another colleague or person that the healthcare professional or executive knows and trusts.

The best way to ensure you'll get a meeting with members on the product evaluation committee is if your champion, coach, or someone that knows the committee member contacts them on your behalf and asks them to give you some of their time. Often, all it takes is a simple phone call and you're in.

Sometimes, the person who knows the committee member, may not want to personally make a call for you. Ask this person if it would be acceptable if you used his or her name when contacting the committee member. That may be all it takes to get your foot in the door.

Suppose you asked Dr. Smith if you can use his name to call Mrs. Peabody, the infection control nurse on the committee. Whether Mrs. Peabody or a secretary answers the phone, you might say, "Hello. My name is Todd Evans from XYZ Vascular. Dr. Smith asked me to give Mrs. Peabody a call. Is she available, please?" This should be all that you need to get Mrs. Peabody on the phone or to have her return your call.

Make sure that you are prepared for the conversation before you call by having clearly defined goals. Do you plan to discuss issues during the call or will you try to set up a face-to-face meeting? Know your talking points before you pick up the phone.

The conversation should focus in on:

- That person's specific concerns and how they are addressed by your product
- Uncovering and handling any objections regarding using your product

Plan each presentation by asking yourself the following question: "What is the pain that can be reduced or eliminated by my product or service for this person's position or department?"

If you cannot think of any direct benefit, your next job is to anticipate any objections this person might raise against using your product or service. Create a written list.

Use a list of solutions your product offers and any anticipated objections to craft your approach. Plan the questions you will ask to get each person to describe associated problems and benefits from their individual perspective.

For example, let's assume that you are selling the pressure-measuring catheter mentioned earlier. Mrs. Peabody needs to know if it meets the infection control standards for an in-dwelling catheter. What questions might she ask you? Let's presume that infection control personnel are normally concerned with the following regarding your product:

- Does the sterile packaging avoid contamination when opened for use?
- Are the instruments to place the catheter single-use disposable or reusable?
- What features does your product have to reduce the possibility of infection?

• Does it meet all other infection control standards for similar products?

List as many questions as you can think of that you might be asked during the call or during a meeting. This way, you won't be caught off-guard.

Once you get Mrs. Peabody on the phone, if your goal is to see her in person, you could say, "Mrs. Peabody, Dr. Smith has requested an evaluation of our pressure catheter. It will be going before the product evaluation committee in a few weeks. There are some infection control features that Dr. Smith is excited about, but he wanted you to see them ahead of the committee meeting. May I meet with you at a convenient time so you may review those features for Dr. Smith?"

If an appointment to meet in person is what you're after, don't try to sell anything besides the appointment. In this case, you related that Dr. Smith wants her to look at the infection-control features. That should get you the appointment, or it might bring you some questions that Mrs. Peabody wants to have answered first. Either way, it gives you an opportunity to familiarize yourself with Mrs. Peabody's concerns and to address them on the call or in person.

What if you are trying to contact a committee member and you need to leave a voicemail message? Make sure you deliver the same information as outlined for a live call, directed at the committee member's specific interests. For example, if you want to meet with Dr. Clark, the chief radiologist, your message might sound something like this:

"Dr. Clark, my name is Todd Evans, with XYZ Vascular. Dr. Smith is interested in evaluating our Easy Place pressure catheter. It will be going before the product evaluation committee in a few weeks and Dr. Smith asked me to contact you ahead of the meeting to ensure that it meets the imaging and safety criteria for your department. Dr. Smith is especially excited that you see our unique feature that allows you to easily verify anatomic placement using plain film, CT imaging or MRI. I promised Dr. Smith that I would schedule time with you as soon as possible so that he could get your feedback. Please contact me at 205-555-5555 to let me know the best way for you to review the product. On behalf of Dr. Smith and myself, I look forward to hearing back from you as soon as possible. Again, my number is 205-555-5555. Thank you. Good-bye."

Did you notice that Dr. Smith's name was mentioned several times during that voicemail? Why? Whose interests do you think Dr. Clark will be more concerned with—yours, or that of his colleague, Dr. Smith? Unless a clinician already has a working relationship with you, he or she usually places salespeople's requests low on the priority list. However, colleagues and staff members take priority, especially as it relates to patient care. Always try to have a medical colleague's name to use when requesting an appointment or trying to get a call back.

Also try to include a WIIFM statement for the person that you are calling. In this instance, we let Dr. Clark know that Dr. Smith is very excited about him seeing the unique feature that allows him to easily verify anatomic placement using any of the common imaging modalities in his department. This suggests that he does not have to change what he is doing—something that almost always plays favorably with physicians and other clinicians.

If you have any difficulty getting through to any of the key people, request help from the end-user that is supporting your product. For example, if you have not received a response from Dr. Clark after several attempts, ask Dr. Smith if he could make a call to Dr. Clark to either have him meet with you or to sign off on the product.

If Dr. Smith reports back to you that he spoke with Dr. Clark, who has given his blessings, then your job with Dr. Clark is just about finished. Out of courtesy, and to avoid any potential problems with Dr. Clark, contact him or leave a voicemail message and summarize the conversation you had with Dr. Smith. Let Dr. Clark know that you are available at any time if he has any questions or needs you to provide him with any information. You don't want the doctor to be able to tell a committee that you never called on him or contacted him.

Keep Accurate Records

One thing that you do not want to have happen at a product evaluation committee meeting is for one of the members to say, "I have no prior knowledge of this product. No one contacted me." It is very uncomfortable to dispute a committee member's claim that you did not attempt to contact them when you did. You won't make friends by replying, "I tried contacting you several times, but you never returned my calls."

I recommend strongly that you maintain an accurate contact record for each and every phone call, e-mail or face-to-face meeting that you have with every person in your territory. This record should include the big five: who, what, where, when, and how.

Who: Who did you speak with? Whether it was a customer, a prospect, an administrative assistant, a receptionist or whoever—get a name.

What: Write down specifically what you discussed with that person and any responses, such as, "I discussed the need to speak with Dr. Smith about the surgery. Agnes said that she will make sure that Dr. Smith gets my message."

Where: Where was this person when you made contact? Was it in the office, clinic, in a specific hospital department, the parking lot, etc.?

When: Record the day, date and time.

How: How did you make contact with this person? Was it through a referral from one of the committee member's colleagues? Did you call on the phone, stop by the office or send a letter, e-mail, or fax?

Should one of the committee members state that you never contacted them, you can then demonstrate to the committee that you did make the effort. You must be tactful when you do this—just as in handling objections, you won't make many friends by proving them wrong. However, you could tactfully say, "Dr. Craig, I'm sorry that you did not receive my message. I spoke with Debbie Jones, the receptionist in your department, at 9:45 a.m. on Tuesday, January 19. I told her that I was calling to speak to you on behalf of Dr. Adams, regarding the product evaluation committee. I also left three voicemails to extension 4192 on January 22, at 8:20 a.m., January 26, at 2:22 p.m., and January 29, at 4:30 p.m. Again, I'm sorry you did not receive my messages, but as you can see, I have made numerous attempts to contact you. Dr. Craig, to avoid any problems in the future, what is the best way for me to contact you directly?"

The person will either stick to the story that he or she did not receive your message or might offer to look into the matter. But you have just demonstrated to the committee that you are detail-oriented and take a professional approach to your business. In your call records, you'll have records of calls that you made and completed to other committee members who can validate the entries. This gives you great credibility, and good record keeping can one day save you from accusations regarding omissions or mistakes.

Be Prepared to Speak about More than Just Your Product

When you are speaking with a product evaluation committee, you are speaking to a group of experts. Each member of the committee is knowledgeable about the issues that concern his or her department. They know products they are currently using and probably are familiar with your competitors.

Be prepared to competently address any and all issues that may arise. For example, you must be thoroughly familiar with all of the competitive products on the market, specifically those products that are being considered besides to yours. In addition to basic product knowledge, you must be capable of discussing the clinical and technical data, including clinical outcomes relating to your product. Make sure that you are familiar with and can address any questions or issues regarding packaging, sterilization and environmental issues.

Benefits that Get Positive Responses

Overall, there are several benefits that will elicit positive responses from product evaluation committees. These include:

- Better documented clinical outcomes
- Saves time
- User-friendly
- Increases safety for staff
- Increases safety for patient
- Reduces risk exposure for hospital
- Product is part of a group purchasing organization (GPO) or contract
- Reduces cost of current product
- Reduces cost of overall procedure or care
- Enhances hospital buying position

- Consolidates and reduces inventory through consignment or just-in-time delivery
- You and your company have an excellent reputation of serving this facility

Any time that you can present information with supportive documentation that substantiates any of the points above, you'll have the positive attention of the committee. Certainly, you will need to address any individual concerns as well, but no healthcare professional can ignore any of the benefits listed above.

One-on-One Meetings versus Group Dynamics

There are advantages and disadvantages to meeting with committee members individually versus meeting with a group. One-on-one meetings usually allow people to more easily speak their minds without inhibition. If anyone is uncomfortable with you or your products or anticipates any problems making a change from what they are currently using, he or she is more likely express it in private.

Although it might be uncomfortable for you, as well as the person you're meeting with, encourage him or her to be honest in expressing any and all feelings regarding the decision to be made. This gives you the opportunity to uncover and handle personal objections that might not be voiced in a group setting. Always try to create and take advantage of this opportunity.

Group presentations with product evaluation committees have their share of pluses and minuses. On the plus side, these presentations tend to be much less emotional, as most people will avoid displaying strong emotions in a group setting. However, you will encounter some drama kings and queens who like to demonstrate how committed they are to the institution with an emotional display. A passionate committee member can affect the group in either a positive or negative way. Be careful not to attack that person's position, because doing so might come across as attacking anyone who shares that person's point of view.

One of the drawbacks of a group setting is that opinions may be stated based on what other people on the committee think. For example, if a person acts as if he or she is not concerned about cost or ease of use for all staff members, then that person will look bad to the materials manager, CFO and nurse educator. So, even if cost is not a personal or departmental concern, a committee member may pretend that it is, just to save face.

Sometimes, personal issues can come into play. I know of a case where a physician objected to a CEO's argument that the doctor did not need a certain product to perform a procedure. The doctor launched a verbal attack on the CEO during a committee meeting, asserting that the CEO was not competent to be a hospital administrator. This turned the group against the doctor, and to some extent, against the sales representative who was then deemed guilty by association. The doctor eventually got his way and the salesperson got his sale, but it took some time for people on the committee to forgive the salesperson for something he didn't do.

Occasionally, someone on a committee may put you in the uncomfortable position of selling the end-user against your product! One time, a purchasing director suggested that she would make things difficult for me if I did not discourage a surgeon from using one of my new products, because of the increased cost to the hospital. I told her that it was not my job to deny any of my company's products or services to a licensed healthcare provider. I told her that the healthcare professional decides what is best for his or her patient and it is strictly

forbidden for me to interfere. If you ever find yourself in a similar situation, I urge you to do the same. As long as you have provided the clinician and facility with the appropriate product information,
including the approved indications and any contraindications for a
product, you have done your job. Suggesting to a doctor or other
healthcare professional how to treat a patient is tantamount to making medical decisions. Sales reps don't make medical decisions.

Be prepared to engage customers both one-on-one and as a group.
Always seek individual meetings with product committee members
and attend any group meetings if you are permitted.

Hints for Getting To and Scoring Points with Hospital Managers and Other Committee Members

- Determine which people in which departments need to be targeted by asking the end-user and other committee members.
- Conduct some research to see how involved each committee
  member will be with respect to your product. Try to determine
  each person's hot buttons, or factors that will most influence a decision, ahead of time.
- Find out how each committee member perceives your company
  and your competitors.
- Offer targeted seminars on topics that committee members need
  to learn more about with respect to your product or services.
- Get your senior management involved directly with the formal
  presentation to the committee. Sometimes, bringing in management shows that this account is not only important to you, but
  also important to your company. Even though it hurts, some hospital managers and clinicians would rather deal with your managers than deal with you. Give them what they want.

- Offer special value added services and educational programs (in-services) for the staff in each department.
- Invite committee members and any associated personnel to tour your company's facilities, if feasible.

Where Does the Money Come From to Pay for Your Products?

One of your goals as a medical sales professional is to get paid. This usually happens once your company gets paid. Where does the money come from to pay for your products? It may come from the *capital budget*, *operational budget* or *patient charge item* category.

Budgets

Budgets serve as guides and controls to spending that help your healthcare customers to achieve operational and performance goals. A process is in place that determines how the overall capital and operational budgets are allocated.

What is the difference between a capital budget and an operational budget?

Capital budgets provide money to support projects and equipment purchases whose useful lives span several years or more. This includes construction of new buildings or renovating existing space, and the acquisition of expensive equipment, such as MRIs, lasers, beds, computer systems, furniture, etc.

The operational budget provides money for recurring items that must be paid on a periodic basis. This includes labor costs, such as employee salaries and benefits; utilities, operational provisions like medical supplies, pharmaceuticals and office supplies; and any other equipment priced below a certain level. Capital equipment maintenance and financing are also funded in the operational budget.

If you sell capital equipment, one concern is getting your product placed into the capital budget. How does this occur?

The capital budget identifies items to be purchased in the upcoming year. Approval is often based on the facility's requirements to expand into new technologies, replace outdated equipment and the associated escalating maintenance costs, plus the facility's plans for expansion. Each department manager submits a capital proposal to the finance department 6-12 months in advance of the time they plan to purchase. In some cases, items for capital purchase may be considered up to three years in advance.

Department managers will often ask their suppliers to submit a proposal for cost, along with any information that may help to get the item approved. This might include:

- A full description of the product
- Justification of why the product is needed
- How the product helps to support the facility's overall goals and mission
- The financial implications of buying vs. not buying the product
- Any implications in terms of ability to increase patient load and reduce employee workload
- How the product will affect the facility from a competitive standpoint in the healthcare market

Who decides what and how do they decide?

Approvals for capital purchases are often decided by committee. The committee may be known as the Budget Review Committee, Capital Review Committee or some other name. It is often composed of C-level executives such as the CEO, CFO, COO, medical chief of staff, board of directors and other hospital staff members.

Hospitals and clinics that are part of a multi-facility organization may need to seek final approval of capital items from the parent organization. Often, this is required when the purchase exceeds a certain amount. Generally, the smaller the facility, the simpler the process in terms of the number of steps to get a capital proposal reviewed.

One thing that the medical sales professional must be aware of is the capital budget cycle for each account in his or her territory. Sales presentations should be planned with respect to the proposal submission date. Proposals must be completed so they can be submitted on time for review. Typical time from submission to final decision averages 4-6 months. If you miss the submission date, you may have to wait a year until it comes around again.

Learn each facility's capital budgeting timeline and use it when formulating your sales plan. Department managers will often explain their facility's capital budget cycle deadlines, if you ask.

It is also critically important that you are able to discuss financing and leasing options for your products, if appropriate. Your company and any finance company that you work with will provide you with the necessary information and how to present it to your customers. Hospitals and clinics often secure their own funding, but anything you can offer that gives your accounts more financing options can help your sale.

Sometimes, capital purchases can be broken down into component parts to qualify for the operational budget. For example, if you sold a set of surgical instruments whose total cost exceeds the threshold for the capital budget, you might be able to sell the set to the hospital, one instrument at a time. Some facilities will allow this, while other won't. You won't know unless you ask.

Find out if your product is considered a patient charge item. These are items that are used one time and get charged separately to the patient. Some hospital departments issue a single charge for a procedure, which includes all items used. This could place some items that are normally patient charge items into the operational budget. It's not always obvious which items are considered patient charge and which are not, so be sure to ask.

Develop Relationships Before You Need Them

Salespeople are good at locating and seeking conversations with the right people in an account when it's necessary. What the medical sales professional does, however, is develop these relationships ahead of need.

C-level executives are not in the normal call pattern for most medical sales. In fact, these busy executives might not give you any of their valuable time without a valid reason. But there are often opportunities to meet these important people over time, and you should always make it a point to know who they are and allow them to know you. Make sure your business card is on file in the executive suite.

Successful medical sales professionals do the things that less successful sales reps often refuse to do. This includes getting to know anyone who could influence a sale at any time in the future. You never know who is going to be promoted into a position with buying power. Developing good relationships with everyone before the sale creates a good feeling about you and your company during the sale.

Summary

As healthcare becomes more complex, so will the process for account penetration. Knowing how to approach and sell the different parties that have any level of decision in approving your products or services is essential. Keep in mind that once you develop a connection with these people, the process becomes easier.

Medical sales professionals who know and understand their accounts inside and out have a competitive advantage. This requires making the extra effort that your competition might not be willing to make. The medical sales environment is changing, and those sales professionals who know how to adapt and change with it will be richly rewarded. Learn how to penetrate your accounts, so that you become the trusted vendor of choice whenever possible.

17

Getting In To See the Doctor—Strategies for Getting Past the Gatekeeper

Whether you call on physicians or not, you will have customers and prospects that are difficult to get in and see. In this chapter, I'll be referring to the doctor, since traditionally, doctors are some of the hardest prospects to schedule time with. But keep in mind that the techniques I describe here should work with almost any of your healthcare prospects.

One of the biggest challenges for new medical sales representatives (and even some of the more seasoned ones) is how to get past the gatekeeper in a doctor's office. The gatekeeper is any of the doctor's employees who control access to the doctor. It could be:

- The receptionist
- The office manager
- The physician's scheduler
- The physician's secretary
- The physician's medical assistant (M.A)
- The physician assistant (P.A.)
- The X-ray tech or other ancillary personnel

Many salespeople struggle getting in the door because they go about it the wrong way. I'm going to cut straight to the chase about what I believe are the best approaches for getting past the gatekeeper, and then I'll mention a few others.

The best way for a salesperson to establish a relationship in any organization is to use a *top-down* approach. This means that you want to establish your relationships as high up in the organization as possible. Why? Basically, there are two reasons:

1. The higher up in the organization someone sits, the greater his or her power to make important decisions without the need to consult with someone else.
2. The level at which a salesperson establishes a relationship in an organization is usually the level where that salesperson tends to interact from then on.

If you only establish a relationship with the receptionist in a doctor's office, you may have a very difficult time moving beyond that level. Am I saying to disregard the usefulness of a relationship with the receptionist? Not at all—I'm just suggesting that you set your target much higher.

How much higher? Why not start at the top? Who has the ultimate say in the doctor's practice 99.99 percent of the time? The doctor. If he decides that he wants to see you in his office, no one is going to stop you. Start with the doctor!

How do you get to the doctor when you need to go through that layer of other people? Well, maybe you don't! If you think that your only approach to the doctor is via the receptionist-secretary-office manager route, then you are thinking like 90 percent of the medical salespeople calling on that doctor, including most of your competition. So, let's explore a few different approaches.

Approach 1: If your product line or service regularly places you in the hospital or medical clinic, then you need to find or create an opportunity to "bump into" the doctor during a time when he is "in the house." There is an art to this, so just don't rush up and launch into a presentation when you locate him.

Obey this important rule: *Do not* approach the doctor if he is engaged in a conversation, treating a patient, writing in a chart or dictating a report. Wait until he has finished his present task and try to catch him in-between activities.

Remember, your aim is not to give a sales presentation, but to try and arrange an appointment or opportunity to discuss your products or services at a convenient time.

Here's how it's done. If you have not yet met the doctor, excuse yourself and tell him who you are: "Excuse me, Dr. Smith—I'm Ted Smith, from XYZ Medical. I have wanted to meet you." Offer your handshake and a smile.

Next, you are going to ask a simple question—"Dr. Smith, who should I speak with in your office to schedule 10 minutes with you?" You may get many different responses at this point. The response that you want is a name. Let's assume he says, "Carol, my scheduler, sets all of my appointments." You will then ask, "May I call Carol and tell her that you and I spoke and ask her to schedule an appointment?" More than likely, the doctor is going to ask you why you want to meet with him, but if he just says, "Sure. Give Carol a call," say "Thank you. I look forward to meeting with you," and move on.

Now, if the doctor does ask, "What are you selling," or "What do you want to discuss?," you need to answer carefully. *How you answer the question may well determine your success or failure in obtaining the appointment.*

When you tell the doctor what you would like to discuss, it needs to be expressed in a way that clearly defines a benefit for the doctor and the doctor's patients. If you answer, "I would like to show you my company's new pacemaker," it sounds like you're just trying to make a sale, which is more of a benefit for you than it is to the doctor. With that approach, there is a good chance that the doctor will respond with, "I already have a pacemaker that I'm happy with. I'm not interested."

If you ask the question in a way that suggests an advantage or potential benefit over what the doctor is currently using, you stand a much better chance of getting the appointment. Ideally, you need to ask a question that has the doctor wanting more information; for example, "Dr. Smith, our new Quickticker 1000 can be programmed in half the time of other pacemakers on the market. This can save you and your patients 30 minutes of O.R. time. Who should I talk to in your office to schedule a 15-minute meeting?" Did you notice the assumptive close for the appointment? You probably have the doctor wondering how you can save him 30 minutes during the procedure and he will hopefully grant you the appointment to find out.

Let's assume that the doctor gives you the name of his scheduler and grants approval to call and set the appointment. Treat that as a directive from the top of his organization, because it is.

Suppose Dr. Smith tells you to call Carol in his office for an appointment. When you call the office to speak with Carol, if anyone asks why you need to speak with her, you simply respond, "Dr. Smith asked me to give Carol a call." That should be all that you need to get her on the phone.

When you are connected to Carol, politely introduce yourself and say, "Carol, I spoke with Dr. Smith at the hospital this afternoon, and he asked me to call you to schedule 15 minutes with him. What day and time looks best to meet with him?" Carol knows that no salesperson is going to be foolish enough to say that the doctor asked him to call unless he did. She will probably confirm the information with the doctor, but *voila* . . . you have your appointment!

Approach 2: I have spoken with many doctors regarding this next technique, and based upon their responses, it is one of the best methods for getting in to see a physician with whom you have not yet established a working relationship.

Nothing will get you a meeting with a doctor faster than a warm referral from someone that he likes and trusts. Who might that be?

One of the strongest referrals you can get is from one of the doctor's colleagues. Ask some of the doctors with whom you have established rapport if they know the doctor you wish to meet with well enough to help you out. Some things that suggest a good working relationship between doctors is when they are associates in the same group, practice the same specialty or refer patients to each other. If the doctor you are seeking a referral from likes your product or service and likes you, there's a good chance he will help you, but be sure that the referring doctor is someone the other doctor respects.

Try to get the name of a contact in the office of the doctor you're trying to get in to see. If the doctor referring you doesn't have the name of a contact, perhaps someone in his office does. Once you have a name, call that person and say, "Hi Mandy, I'm calling on behalf of Dr. Smith, who asked me to call you to schedule an appointment with Dr. Adams." Are you starting to see the way this works? When you tell employees that you are calling because "the boss" or another doctor asked you to, the response is usually much different than what you would expect from an ordinary cold call.

Another person who can refer you to a specific doctor is a sales representative who has an established relationship with that doctor and sells products that do not compete with yours. Sales reps know each other's reputations, so as long as you are regarded as someone of integrity and good character, you may be able to structure a *quid pro quo* arrangement. You will help the other rep to get appointments with doctors with whom you enjoy a good relationship and he or she will do the same for you. Remember that other salespeople you recommend to your customers will reflect upon you, so choose them carefully.

Approach 3: Send the doctor a personal letter that spells out, in the first line, *what's in it for him and his patients* when he meets with you. While many sales reps send letters and write notes, it's usually the same, "I would like to come by and show you our new blah, blah, blah," without ever giving the prospect a single reason why he should be interested. Send only benefit-driven letters, or you will come across like every other sales rep who is just trying to make a sale. Don't forget to mention in the letter that you will be calling his office in the next day or so to speak with the person who schedules his appointments, so could he please authorize her to schedule X minutes with you to show him how he could [review the benefits]. The letter should be written on personal stationary, not company letterhead, and marked "Personal and Confidential" on the front.

It may be tempting to use e-mail instead of traditional snail mail, but I caution you not to unless the prospect has suggested that you use e-mail to communicate with him. It just takes a quick click on the delete button for your message to be gone. Also, many doctors consider e-mail their personal domain and if you send it when you have not been invited to do so, you are spamming. A spammer will be viewed as more of a nuisance than an asset.

Approach 4: This is a good approach to use after sending a letter as in Approach 3, but it also works well on its own. Before approaching the receptionist, prepare a handwritten note that spells out the benefits that the doctor will get from meeting with you, and request to speak with him while you are in the office. Approach the receptionist and say, "Hi Barbara, I'm Todd Smith from XYZ Medical, could you please let Dr. Blake know that I'm here to speak with him, and could you please hand him this?" Hand her the folded note. If she tells you that the doctor is busy, just say, "I understand. Would you please hand him the note and let him know that I'm here. If he doesn't have time to meet with me, I'll understand, but he needs to know that I'm here." Again, make sure you specifically state in the note what's in it for the doctor (WIIFM) if he meets with you—don't just write that you would like to show him one of your products.

The key with all of these approaches is to be pleasantly and professionally persistent. If your initial attempts fail, get better at defining your benefits message and keep trying. Don't be afraid to mix up the approaches and don't give up. Once the doctor realizes that he or his patients may benefit, he'll meet with you.

If you are unable to communicate directly with the doctor, then you will need to go through other office personnel, but don't waste time talking to the wrong people. Find out who the true gatekeeper is. How? Just ask!

Too many medical sales representatives never get past the receptionist, because one of the receptionists main jobs, besides greeting patients and answering the phone, is to keep salespeople away from the doctor. It's amazing that some medical sales professionals allow their futures to be controlled by the lowest-paid employee in the doctor's office. Don't misunderstand me—always treat the receptionist with respect and kindness—she is just doing her job, and is in a position to help you if she wants to. Don't allow the receptionist to be the last stop in your quest for a face-to-face meeting with the doctor.

The next time you are confronted by a receptionist who denies you access to the back office, politely ask, "I know you are busy, and I don't want to take up your valuable time in the future with similar requests. Could you please tell me who would be the best person to speak with to schedule time with Dr. Blake?" She may suggest you speak with one of the other staff members. Ask if that person is available for you to speak with at that moment, or what the best time is to reach that person by phone.

Your long-term goal is to eventually develop the type of relationship in which you can meet with the doctor whenever you need to. This requires you to also develop a good working relationship with the people who work closely with the doctor on a day-to-day basis. While you're at it, strive to build solid, friendly relationships with anyone and everyone in the office who will champion your cause, by passing along the message that you are a nice person and a true professional.

Here's a valuable tip. Initially, if you are unable to get in to see the doctor, and the doctor works with a physician's assistant (P.A.), see about making an appointment with the P.A. and discussing the benefits of your product or service with him or her. P.A.'s might not be able to make the decision to try your offering on their own, but they can sell the doctor on the idea if they see the benefits. Most work very closely with their attending physicians and help influence the doctor's thinking. Don't overlook this important player's role in achieving the sale.

Getting past the gatekeeper to see the doctor is not as difficult as it seems if you understand the players involved and have the courage to try some different approaches. The keys are to always be polite and professional, don't step on anyone's toes and don't become a nuisance. Get the doctor to see you as a *benefit* to his practice instead of an *interruption*. That is the ticket to having unlimited access to the doctors in your territory.

Reasons Medical Sales Reps Don't Get an Appointment with the Doctor

- They don't generate enough interest
- They don't provide enough value
- They don't create or uncover the need
- They don't establish rapport
- They "tell," instead of "sell"
- The doctor sees your offering as low priority
- The doctor feels you were more focused on your problem (the need to sell) than his practice and his patients
- The doctor has an unfavorable impression of you, your company or your product

18

Medical Sales During Tough Financial Times

One factor that compels people to enter medical sales is that healthcare has always been one of the strongest industries in the U.S. economy. Regardless of what is happening in the world, people will always become sick and injured. There will always be a demand for medical care, along with a need for the associated equipment, supplies and services.

While healthcare is considered recession resistant, it is not recession-proof. Pullbacks in the economy eventually trickle down to those who provide healthcare products and services. When business is good and there is money in the bank, along with available credit to help finance purchases, healthcare institutions and providers reinvest in new equipment and supplies. Likewise, when economic conditions strain the bottom line for healthcare institutions, there tends to be a pullback in spending.

When this book was first published in 2010, the U.S. economy was in the worst shape since the great depression and healthcare was feeling its share of the misery. In this type of economy, there are three main economic issues affecting healthcare providers.

One major problem is unemployment. The effect of this is obvious—no job, no paycheck. People who have lost their insurance benefits avoid going to the doctor. Many cannot afford expensive co-pays, even if they still have health insurance. Elective surgical procedures get postponed. Patients are using the Emergency Room for primary treatment and not paying their bills. The bottom line is that hospitals are operating in the red and looking to cut costs anywhere they can. This includes canceling or postponing capital purchases and buying commodity items at the lowest prices possible.

The next problem is a lack of available credit. It is not as easy as it once was for healthcare providers and institutions to tap into credit lines or borrow money to finance the purchase of equipment, supplies and services. Without money on hand or the ability to borrow, nonessential new equipment purchases get deferred until things improve.

The last problem is that hospitals and other healthcare providers have lost money on investments, just like every other business and the general public. This means that funds that were previously available have shrunken or disappeared.

Under these circumstances, how do you, the medical sales professional, continue to sell your products and services?

Regardless of the Economy, Do What You Are Paid To Do

Your job is to sell your company's products and services, period. That's how you get paid. That's how your company stays in business.

In tough economic times, selling is more of a challenge. Financial concerns can supersede clinical needs because a hospital or clinic can't treat patients if it can't meet its payroll and pay its bills. The power to make buying decisions shifts more from the end-user to one or more executives and managers that decide how to allocate funds.

As a medical sales professional, you can't afford to sit back and wait for things to improve. Opportunities exist for you to sell your products, but they may not be as obvious as in good economic times. You must find these opportunities or create them. Your current work habits will determine your income and your future in this business.

Here's why you need to work harder than ever:

- If you are a sales professional on commission, your paychecks are going to be pretty lean if you're not closing business. You didn't enter the medical sales profession to earn a meager income and just get by. Keep your income goals high!

- Your company is in business to sell products or services, and if you're not getting the job done, they will replace you with someone who can. Forget about what you have done in the past, because your company already has. They are only interested in what you are selling this week, this month or this quarter, because they can't meet their financial goals and pay their bills with your past performance.

- Your competition might see this as an opportunity to eat your lunch. While you're in the office, licking your wounds, they are out looking for ways to sell their products to *your* accounts any way they can. It doesn't look good when you've told your company that doing business with XYZ hospital is impossible and one of your competitors lands the account.

- How you operate as a medical sales professional now will impact your business in the future when things improve.

The reality is that in any sales position you need to, "sell what you've got to the customers that you've got." In good times or bad, you need to move forward and uncover the opportunities that are out there. If you can't find them, go create them. Waiting for better times is not an option.

A Bad Economy Won't Last Forever— Neither Will A Good Economy

When budgets are tight, keep in mind that it won't last forever. If your products and services are progressive and needed, your customers will buy, in time. But the time to act is now, because you still need to eat now. There is also a high likelihood that your customers need what you sell now and they need to get it from someone. Why not you?

Taking positive and continuous action in a crisis defines you as a person and as a sales professional. Consider how your actions look through the eyes of your customers—the companies and sales professionals who engage and counsel them in bad times often get first shot at their business when times improve. Everything you do matters, regardless of the state of the economy. The only time you win in sales is when you sell something. If your customers can't buy now, your job is to stay on their radar screens, so you'll be front and center when they decide to buy.

Don't forget to pay attention to your personal finances. To some, that means earning as much commission as you can whenever you can, but that's not good enough. During good times, make sure you set some money aside for when times are not so good. One thing that can ruin good salespeople is having their own finances suffer. It's hard to stay focused on business when you can't keep up with your own bills. Salespeople with financial problems often come off as desperate and too anxious to make a sale. You don't want to find yourself in this situation.

Create a financial cushion to get you through periods of slow sales or even unemployment. It's easy to get caught up in splurging when times are good. Just know that everything changes—including the economy, your customers' buying habits and your own financial needs. Stash cash for the rainy days, because selling in healthcare involves many variables and sooner or later, it's going to rain. You should have enough money set aside to get you through a minimum of six months of living expenses.

Know Why Your Customer's Are Not Buying
or
Why They Are Not Buying From You!

With tight budgets and a falling economy, it might seem obvious why your customers are not buying. If you dig no deeper than your own assumptions, you could be leaving a lot of money on the table. Ask yourself how your customers are currently allocating money for products and services. If they have delayed or cancelled a purchase, find out why. What are their intentions regarding your products and services in the future? What can you do to help ensure you will eventually get the sale or shorten the delay?

Make no mistake—if there is a demand for healthcare, there is a need for products and services. Don't just walk away when a customer tells you that they're not buying. If their doors are open for business, they still need supplies, equipment and services to function. They also can't ignore anything that improves their operational efficiency to save money or make money. Find out what they are buying, how they are buying it and from whom. Look for ways to have them buy from *you*.

Don't just accept excuses such as, "The hospital has delayed all capital expenditures," or "There is a mandate that the institution use the lowest priced products that are acceptable to the product evaluation committee." Start searching for any hidden opportunities by talking to the players involved.

Go to Your Coach and Champion

When you are facing strong buying resistance, due to politics or a tight budget, find someone of influence to champion your cause, plus a knowledgeable insider to coach you through the system. This could be several people or just one.

There are often a number of employees and healthcare professionals who decide on buying products and services. In order to find out who is involved with yours and gain access to them, you're going to need help. Your coach and champion can tell you who these people are and help you determine each party's position regarding your product or service.

If the sum total of decision-makers don't perceive a need for your product or service, they won't be buying. Your job is to change that perception and to help them find ways to buy what you sell. That's what a medical sales professional does.

Identify the Players, Then Define Their WIIFM

Selling in any economy requires that you address each buyer's WIIFM. Find out what it is.

Harry Mifflin sells surgeon-controlled surgical robots. He has been working for almost a year to get his surgical robot into XYZ Medical Center.

Dr. Jones, a staff urologist, is trained to use the robot for minimally invasive prostatectomy procedures. He is one of the main proponents of the surgical robotic technology at the hospital.

Dr. Edwards, a new cardiothoracic surgeon on staff, did a one-year fellowship in minimally invasive cardiac procedures, including minimally invasive robotic coronary artery bypass surgery. He believes the robot is the key to the hospital remaining competitive in the community.

Everything was looking great for Harry's sale until the hospital felt the crunch of the economy and the capital budget was frozen indefinitely. The director of purchasing told Harry not to expect a purchase order any time soon. The robot, which had been a priority for several months, had fallen to the bottom of the list as the hospital went into survival mode.

Should Harry attempt to salvage the sale or just sit back and lament his bad luck for the next year or two?

Harry needs to know where his product lies with respect to the budget committee's priorities. He begins with those people who would like to have his product the most—the surgeons, Dr. Jones and Dr. Edwards.

Harry meets with Dr. Jones. He discusses the challenges that the doctor faces growing his practice and what's in it for the doctor and his patients (WIIFM) if the hospital gets the robot.

Dr. Jones is very disappointed with the hospital's decision to delay the purchase. He has been losing patients to a urology group across town that already uses a robot at a competing hospital. That hospital's marketing program has made patients aware of the benefits of minimally invasive surgery, including less pain and fewer complications. The robot has been part of the strategic marketing plan for Dr. Jones's practice, and now he is faced with a choice. He can continue to support XYZ medical center and accept the loss of patients, or he can apply for staff privileges at the hospital across town and offer the minimally invasive procedure to his patients.

Harry asks Dr. Jones if he could coach him in terms of defining the WIIFM for the other players involved with the purchase. With Dr. Jones's help, Harry comes up with the following list:

• Operating Room Manager—Betty Blue, R.N.

WIIFM for Ms. Blue and her department: increased surgical cases and revenue for the department create a larger capital budget and operational budget, which means being able to purchase new equipment for other specialties and hire more personnel. Also, Betty has been pushing to add an addition on to the O.R. for the last four years. The increased schedule for prostate surgery and cardiac surgery would help to support her agenda.

• Medical Chief of Staff—Dr. Tim Howard, M.D.

WIIFM for Dr. Howard and the rest of the medical staff: XYZ medical center has always been regarded as a second tier player for modern technology. Dr. Howard has had difficulty attracting new doctors to the hospital because they consider it low-tech and fear their patients will opt for the more modern hospital across town. Having the robot and being able to offer 21st century minimally invasive procedures would help put the hospital on an equal footing with the competing hospital for physician recruitment.

• Hospital CEO—Ed Rodgers

WIIFM for Mr. Rodgers and XYZ Medical Center: Mr. Rodgers's agenda in recent years has included modernizing outdated equipment in the hospital. He knows that being competitive means recruiting new physicians at the same rate as the hospital across town. Reimbursements for minimally invasive procedures are profitable and would increase the hospital's bottom line. Increasing the surgical volume on profitable cases would allow the hospital to move less profitable cases to an outpatient surgery center. The new robotic procedures will align nicely with the hospital's proposed public relations and marketing campaign that is a priority to fund once economic conditions improve. The hospital may also qualify for a new state healthcare technology grant that can be used to subsidize indigent patients who require the new technology, again adding to the bottom line.

Knowing the WIIFM for each player allows Harry to brainstorm possible approaches and solutions to try and bring the sale back to life. Even when capital budgets are frozen, hospitals still need to boost profits and prevent the loss of paying patients to competitors.

What can Harry do?

The following are some hypothetical ideas worth exploring with the personnel listed above. Harry must prepare a cost justification argument that favors the hospital getting the robot now as opposed to waiting. To accomplish this, he must:

- Get from Dr. Jones a conservative estimate of the number of minimally invasive prostatectomy procedures he could schedule over the next 12 months. What increase in procedures does this represent over what he currently performing at XYZ Hospital?
- Talk to Dr. Edwards to get an estimate of the number of minimally invasive coronary bypass procedures he could schedule over the next 12 months. What increase in procedures does this represent for XYZ Hospital?

- Talk to Dr. Howard, the medical chief of staff, to determine if any additional surgeons could be recruited to the medical staff by having the robot available. If so, ask him to give an estimate of the number of procedures these surgeons would bring to the hospital each month and the types of procedures.
- Ask Ms. Blue to estimate the number of robotic procedures that would be performed monthly, based on the information from Dr. Jones, Dr. Edwards and Dr. Howard.
- Ask Ms. Blue if she can compute the net income increase for the O.R., based on the additional procedures performed each month (Note: check with your company to find out to what extent if any you can assist with the calculations. Corporate compliance issues may limit the information that you can provide to a customer with respect to billing and reimbursement).
- Ask Ms. Blue to present the information to Mr. Rodgers, the hospital CEO.
- Get an appointment to speak with Mr. Rodgers to try and resurrect the sale.

Harry is prepared to discuss different purchasing options to make it easier for the hospital to buy. These include:

- A six-year lease with $0 payments for the first 12 months
- Zero-interest financing for 24 months with no down payment

A minimum monthly purchase agreement of disposable supplies for the robot that enable the hospital to get the robot without a capital investment for one year. An escalating annual payment is made in years two through five to allow the hospital to create revenue in advance to pay for the device.

These examples are hypothetical, but I'm suggesting that you find every option available, in hopes that one or more of them resonates with the hospital's decision-makers. Make it easy for them to say "Yes."

Get Your Champions to Do Your Selling

It's certainly helpful to have champions pave your way by getting you information and persuading key hospital personnel to meet with you, but what if you could get your champions do the actual selling? The institution and its personnel might not be able to share sensitive information with you, but they will with their staff. During good times and bad, a champion can be the most effective weapon in your arsenal.

The key to having a good champion/salesperson is to arm them with the necessary information and give them some tips on how to present it. Remember that most clinicians and department managers are not salespeople and could benefit from your sales expertise.

Advise them to begin their sales presentation with a discussion about the general problem. This would lead to talking about the implications of solving the problem, versus the status quo. Your champion should present your product or service as the solution. Prepare him or her to handle any anticipated objections and to offer some "What if," possibilities.

For example, let's say Dr. Jones is having a conversation with Mr. Rodgers, the hospital CEO. Mr. Rodgers acknowledges that offering minimally invasive procedures would increase the revenue at XYZ Medical Center and make them more competitive with the hospital across town. Without taking steps to modernize and be more competitive, XYZ Medical Center will lag behind the other hospital. But there is no money available in the budget to buy the robotic system at the current time.

Dr. Jones asks the "What if," question. "*What if* we can get the robot for one year with no capital outlay? I spoke with Harry Mifflin, who said he could give us the robot to use for one year if we buy the disposables for 12 cases each month. Dr. Edwards is sure that he can book at least six bypass procedures and I can easily schedule eight to 10 prostatectomies myself. I checked with Ms. Blue and she calculated that the reimbursement for those procedures would provide more than enough money to begin paying the capital expense in year two. The robot will pay for itself! How can we make this happen?"

Could you have the same conversation with Mr. Rodgers? Probably, but it won't have near the impact of a valued staff member saying the same thing.

It is always a good approach to use all of your available resources when trying to make a sale, but *it is critical during tough times.*

Always Focus on the Customer's Solvable Problems

Reimbursements, budgets and the economy are always reasons that customers will use not to buy. Maybe you have programs that can sidestep these issues or not. But there must be other pressing problems that your product or service can solve that will make a difference for the institution, the provider and the patient. It comes down to having the right conversation with each person involved.

Even when money is tight, hospitals and clinics will try to find ways to invest in solutions that offer a rapid return on investment, increase operational efficiency and save money on associated costs, such as energy and insurance. If your product or service *makes money, saves money, saves time, offers the patient a better result* or *reduces risk*—you have something to talk about in any economy.

Always present your product in a way that demonstrates its ability to solve the problem of the specific people or department that you're addressing, and you have a shot at winning them over. As I have stated, selling to a medical institution is often like a candidate soliciting votes in an election—you need to convince one voter at a time. The way to do that is to show empathy for each person's problem and convince them that you can solve it and create a better situation.

Keep Working Toward Future Sales

Healthcare is not going away and bad times don't last forever. As medicine and medical technology evolves, healthcare providers and institutions must update their equipment and treatment options. *If your customers are not buying now, they will be in the future.* When that time comes, they will look to those vendors that have counseled them, supported them and remained visible throughout the years. What you do each day is not just for a current sales effort, but for every sale in the future.

If you have done all that you can do and it is not possible for your customer to buy now, keep working for the time when they can. A down economy last only so long. Budgets won't be frozen forever. Credit will eventually become more available.

You are a medical sales professional. Your job is to help your customers provide care for their patients through the products and services your company offers. Help your customers to get what they want, and you will get what you want.

Remember, healthcare doesn't take a break when the economy does. Stay focused on selling your products and services and you will survive and prosper throughout the ups and downs in your career.

Outwork and Outsmart the Competition

Throughout this book, I have focused on the behaviors and skills of the high income earners in healthcare sales. You must be fully prepared for every engagement, articulate your thoughts clearly, know the clinical environment, understand how healthcare professionals think, and know how to appeal to the WIIFM in each of your customers. Even with all of these critical success skills, nothing will happen in your medical sales career, unless *you* make it happen.

Having the right knowledge isn't enough. Medical sales requires hard work. How hard? Well, if you want to earn what the top producers in your territory are paid, you must know what they do every day to grow their business, and then do at least as much as they do just to compete. However, if your goal is to outsell your competition, you are going to need to work harder and smarter than they do.

Consider for a moment, how your competitors see you and your business. If you have any mutual customers who are using your products, your competitor's goal is to get them to stop ordering what you sell and to replace it with whatever they sell. In those accounts where your competitors have the business, they know that your goal is to replace their products with yours. The more successful you become, the bigger the target is that the competition paints on your back, and when you are gunning for their business, they will voraciously defend it. This probably sounds a bit like war, and it is. The question is, are you willing to do whatever it takes to win the business and then hold onto it?

Medical sales is extremely competitive, if for no other reason than the amount of money that is at stake. A good account can yield five or six figures in commission dollars. That alone is a huge motivator to go after the competition, but I've learned that successful medical sales professionals do it for another reason—they hate to lose because they are very competitive people.

Most sales representatives have a healthy respect for their competition, at least so as not to underestimate them. But some see their competitors as the enemy and make it their personal mission to destroy them. That might work for some, but good competition forces you to be your best. My competitors were one of the key reasons I got out of bed early every morning and worked on my business well into the night. It pays to know as much as you can about the people and companies that you're competing against.

Know Your Competitors

Learn all that you can about your competition. Gather intelligence from any and all sources including customers, anyone who knows them, and by talking to your competitors directly. That's right, talk to them! There are medical reps that walk around with a chip on their shoulders about the competition, even refusing to acknowledge a greeting in a sophomoric attempt to psyche them out. It doesn't work.

Whenever I ran into one of my competitors, I saw it as an opportunity to get to know that person and get a feel for his or her personality. I would be so kind and so nice that even the toughest of the tough would eventually succumb to my efforts and at least talk to me. It's amazing how much you can learn about someone through ordinary conversation and asking a few seemingly innocent questions. I learned where my competitors lived, what time they got up in the morning, the names of their spouses and children, previous employment, what their hobbies were and more. Why? Because I wanted to know what I was up against, and also wanted to know how to get them talking. Even in a seemingly innocent discussion about sports, some competitors might share some valuable information. Occasionally, they would tell me things about their products and mutual customers that they should not have told me. What would I do with the information? Usually nothing, but sometimes, it would reveal some sales opportunities. For example, there were competitors who would tell me when a customer was having a problem with a mutual competitor's product. I might talk to that customer to offer my product as an alternative. But I have never used anything of a personal nature about one of my competitors to increase my chances of making a sale, and neither should you—it can blow up in your face. Let me give you an example.

One of my competitors had a serious drug problem. During a cocktail party at a medical meeting, to which all the participating vendors were invited, John glibly shared stories about his recent drug rehabilitation experience. Tim, another competitor, thought he could increase his own sales opportunities by waging a smear campaign and informing every customer he knew about John's drug problem. The sad truth is that he did some damage to John's reputation, but in time, it would damage Tim's reputation even more. Tim was gleefully sharing the information about John's drug problem with a customer who was the medical chief of staff in Tim's biggest account. As it turned out, the doctor was not only a close personal friend of John's, but also had received treatment for a similar drug problem. The doctor was rightfully appalled that Tim would try to misuse the information about John. The doctor started his own campaign to punish Tim by getting most of his colleagues to stop using Tim's products at the hospital. Tim paid dearly for his unethical conduct.

You may learn personal information about a competitor and it might prove tempting to share that information with customers in the hopes of it harming the competitor's business. Don't do it. Instead, take the high road. Use the information to figure out how you can outsell the competitor in an ethical way. Remember, conversations with customers should be about your products or services and how they can help the healthcare provider and the patient—not about your competitors' personal vices and shortcomings.

Work Habits

What are your work habits? What time do you roll out of bed in the morning? What do you do in the morning to prepare for the day? What time do you show up at your first account and are you fully prepared to engage the customer? On a Friday afternoon at 4:45 p.m., are you still making sales calls or starting your weekend early?

There are successful medical sales professionals who don't have the best selling skills or great personalities, but they succeed by working harder than their competition. It's pretty simple—all things being equal, the sales person who makes more sales calls will sell more. Your highest priority must be spending as much time as possible selling to your customers face-to-face.

The hard work of medical sales doesn't take place only when you're in the field. Winning requires that you know more about your industry and your customers than your competition. You might want to relax and watch television in the evenings or on the weekend, but if there is information you need to learn, this is the time to learn it—not on workdays when you should be in front of your customers selling. Continuing education is a part of medical sales, and successful sales reps make time for it.

If you want to outsell the competition, a great place to start is by taking better control of your own time. Time management is an essential skill for the medical sales professional, but too often a rep's schedule controls him or her instead of the other way around. My corporate clients have said that learning effective time management skills yields one of the highest returns on investment for medical sales people. On average, attendees to our workshops are able to recover one hour each day that they can use to focus on essential tasks. Most sales reps will use this time to make one to two additional sales calls per day on average. That's twenty to forty additional sales calls per month! Do you think that these additional sales calls translate into additional sales and commission dollars?

Time is money! When you wake up earlier, start your workday sooner, manage your time more efficiently, and make more sales calls than your competitors do, the chances are good that you will outsell them. The selling skills covered in this book will certainly improve your closing ratios, but when you add good work habits and time management skills that put you in front of more potential customers, you can become unbeatable.

Invest in Your Business

Don't skimp on the tools, training, and personnel you need to succeed.

Some medical sales reps are responsible for purchasing their own equipment and instrumentation to sell and service their customers. Don't ever try to save money by not having the essential tools and supplies that you need to do your job. Make sure you have backup equipment and product inventory, or know where you can get your hands on them in a hurry so you and your customers don't become sidelined if a piece of equipment should fail, or you need additional product. If it makes good business sense to invest in equipment for your job, that is, if it can make you money, or save you money (i.e., save you from losing a customer)—buy it.

Money invested on education and training will always be money well spent. The best medical sales professionals empower themselves through an ongoing personal development program. They attend seminars and medical meetings that allow them to become and remain experts in their fields. The art and science of medicine is continuously evolving. A specific treatment approach that was considered current six months ago, may be viewed as outdated today. It is essential that you keep your information base up to date. If your company doesn't provide or pay for continuing education, invest in it on your own.

I would attend several medical conferences and industry events each year at my own expense to keep up with current medical trends that related to my products. My clinical customers were hungry for this information as well, but often were too busy to attend the same meetings. A tactic I used to build credibility and get appointments was to prepare a written summary of journal articles and references from the conferences and then call customers' offices and request a meeting to discuss the main "take-away" messages. This almost always landed me an appointment, and in time, positioned me as a useful resource. When customers were searching for a product to solve a problem, many would call me first since they believed I could tell them where to find it. It often created a sales opportunity as well, which is why you want your customers calling *you* first, instead of one of your competitors. Create your own continuing education program so you can become a useful resource to your customers.

Finally, recognize that you can't be two places at the same time, no matter how hard you try. There are customer, corporate, and regulatory responsibilities that can eat into your sales time. Top producers jealously protect that sales time. Just hiring one person to manage inventory, make deliveries, do paperwork, and handle customer service tasks can allow you to earn enough extra commission dollars to pay for that employee many times over. If your company will hire and pay this person– great! But if not, see what is required for you to hire and pay someone on your own. If your company allows it, and it makes good business sense, do it!

Be More Professional Than the Competition

I have already discussed professional dress and behavior in another chapter, but it's worth mentioning again. Always dress professionally for the task that you're engaged in, whatever it is.

A professional arrives early and double-checks that everything needed to give a presentation, deliver an in-service (teaching clinical personnel how to properly use your product), or provide a product or service to a customer is available and functioning properly. This includes having product information and procedure protocols available to refer to if a question should arise. A professional also knows who to call when the customer has a question that he can't answer.

The importance of professional behavior and appearance cannot be overstated. Healthcare providers seek to do business with those who present themselves professionally. Everything you do to reinforce your professionalism makes you a better choice to do business with.

Know What Your Competitors Are Doing, Then Do It Better

Remember, you're goal is not to be as good as your competitors— your goal is to surpass them. Learn what your competitors do for their customers, and then do more. Find out what your competitors know about your industry, and then learn more. Know your competitors' products at least as well as they do and make sure that no competitor or customer knows more about your products than you do.

Your income level in medical sales will be directly proportional to how smart you work and how hard you work. Be grateful if you have competitors who keep you motivated every day. Competition comes with the territory—learn how to use it to your advantage.

20

Medical Sales 2.0—Using the Internet and Social Media

The basics of selling and customer service won't change over time, but the ways that we engage our customers will; in fact, they are changing right now. Healthcare manufacturers and their sales people are communicating with customers and potential customers through the use of the Internet and social media. For some, implementing these technologies has been fairly easy, while others have either struggled or resisted. It is human nature to defy change, especially in the business world where time is money and change consumes that valuable time. Many recognize that change offers the potential for positive outcomes, but there is often a fear that the associated learning curve may cause things to not go as well as expected. If a new approach doesn't work as well as the old, it can mean a loss of customers and income. On the other hand, those who are slow to embrace a new way of doing things may find themselves trailing behind the early adopters.

One of the biggest challenges faced when employing new technologies is how to integrate them with your current systems and processes. For example, the first time I looked at *LinkedIn*, one of the biggest business social media sites in the United States and around the world, I thought, "This is pretty cool, but what do I do with it?" As time progressed, I received requests to *connect* but I still could not answer the *what's in it for me* question as to why I should even bother. I have always considered myself fairly savvy when it comes to technology, but I must confess that it took several years until I realized the benefit of those connections and how to use *LinkedIn* effectively.

I was conducting a product-selling workshop for a surgical sales team when Bob, one of the sales associates, asked my advice regarding a situation with one of his accounts. The hospital was denying its surgeons the use of Bob's products because of pricing issues. Bob was working diligently with his distributor to try and negotiate a mutually acceptable pricing agreement. I asked Bob to describe the attitudes of the hospital personnel involved in the negotiations. Bob said, "I sent Steve, the purchasing agent, a message about the pricing on *Facebook* this morning and . . . " I was stunned! I stared at Bob in disbelief and said, "*Facebook*? You're negotiating a million dollar supply contract on *Facebook*? Are you kidding me?"

In case you live in a cave somewhere or have never connected to the Internet, *Facebook* is a social media site that helps people to connect with each other and share information, photographs, videos, music, and more. For many, it has become the preferred way of staying in touch with everyone they know. I had only used it to communicate with friends and never considered using it for work. When Bob told me that he was using *Facebook* to discuss a crucial business matter, I initially thought he was crazy.

Bob looked at me matter-of-factly and said, "Yeah, *Facebook*. Steve always contacts me on *Facebook*. He even sends me purchase orders through *Facebook*. That's how Steve likes to communicate with sales reps." The whole social media thing started to make sense to me at that moment. It's not just the way that we communicate with friends and family that is changing, but also the way that we do business. This goes beyond using the search engines on the Internet to find providers of goods and services. It is about discovering and creating networks, and understanding how to use those networks to build and support your business. If you have a customer that wants to communicate with you via *Facebook* or any other legitimate method that does not breach privacy issues or violate corporate compliance issues, so be it. If a customer wants to meet with you personally, you show up. If they ask you to call at a specific time, you call. If they ask you to fax a document, email it, or to have it delivered by courier, you comply with that request. As sales people, we try to give our customers what they want, when they want it, and how they want it. Social media offers additional communication options that are very powerful.

Medical Sales 2.0 is the use of web technology to sell, service, and educate your customers. Not all of your customers will be early-adopters of these technologies, but you will have more opportunities to educate, impress, and create interest in your products with those who are.

Tell Your Customers What They Want to Know and Tell Them What You Want Them to Know

Is there anything about you that you wish your customers knew, but if you just came out and told them, it would make you sound like a pompous jerk? For example, let's say that you graduated from a prestigious university *summa cum laude* with a 3.96 GPA, you have extensive experience working in the clinical specialty to which you sell, you do volunteer work with a charity or community service organization, you played football in college, you excel at golf, or just about anything else that makes you stand out in a positive way—don't you wish your prospects and customers knew about it? Perhaps you work some things about yourself into your sales conversations such as, "When I worked as a critical care nurse, I used to . . . " That way, you can position yourself as having relevant knowledge and experience. But would you ever say during a sales conversation, " . . . and by the way, I know these statistics are accurate because I was Phi Beta Kappa at Princeton and I am a member of Mensa (an organization of people whose I.Q. is in the top two percent of the population)." Most people would never say that because such self-aggrandizement is not well perceived by others. But nevertheless, it would be nice if they knew.

Pharmaceutical sales representatives are familiar with the concept of a professional portfolio or "brag book." This is a collection of written proof, photographs and testimonials that allows a sales representative to display his or her industry accomplishments to potential employers. Social media sites and personal web pages can function as a brag book for you to tell your customers about yourself, and if you have never considered an online presence, you may want to.

Successful selling requires that you differentiate your product, your company, and yourself from the competition. It's your job to distinguish your product during sales conversations, and customers can learn about your company online. But where can customers and potential customers view information about *you* that clearly portrays you in a way that benefits you and your business?

You may be thinking, "I'm already on *Facebook*, *LinkedIn*, and *Twitter* plus I have posted 126 videos to *YouTube*—I'm all set!" Just being a member of any of these social media sites won't necessarily help your business. In fact, if there is anything on your pages that a customer or potential customer might perceive as negative, your social media postings could adversely affect your relationships with those customers, cost you your job, or worse! In Chapter 5, *Everything You Do Matters*, I talked about how seemingly harmless information or misperceptions can harm your business. Social media and the Internet now give you and others the opportunity to broadcast information about you, your beliefs and activities to the world. If you sell in the healthcare arena, make sure you consider the potential ramifications of anything you post before you click the "submit" button.

Social Media and the Internet in Healthcare: Regulatory and Compliance Issues

First, let's cut to the chase with some good advice to help keep you out of trouble. It's generally okay to post things about yourself on social media sites and other Internet web sites providing you use good judgment and don't make any comments or display any behavior (in photos or videos) to embarrass yourself or the companies you represent. *However, I strongly recommend you do not post any information about your company, or any products or services you represent without prior written approval from your company.*

In healthcare, you must be ever mindful of the regulatory and compliance issues that dictate what you can say about your products, and how you say it. Making a simple public comment online such as "our drug is better than their drug" can cause you and your company a lot of grief if a regulatory agency decides that you violated one of its rules. For example, if you represent a particular drug, and then comment on a social media site about how well that drug works, the U.S. Food and Drug Administration may argue that you are promoting the drug. Hence, your post could be considered as *promotional material.* An FDA rule regarding promotional materials for pharmaceuticals requires that promotional materials balance any favorable information about a drug such as its efficacy with information about risk. Could such a simple comment come back and bite you? Technically, it could. Your best course of action is to avoid online comments about any of your products or services. Medical device, biotechnology, and pharmaceutical companies are required to be familiar with all FDA regulations and any rule changes that affect sales and marketing. Leave the promotional comments, pictures, graphics, and videos to the manufacturers of the products you represent.

Using the Internet and Social Media to Represent Yourself

People have a natural curiosity about others that they know, or are considering doing business with. While your prospects and customers might not ask specific questions regarding your education, work history, awards, and the like, it is very compelling for them to view the information if it is right in front of them. You can lead customers to your information by inviting them to "connect," "friend," or whatever the specific term is for linking with you online, or by just putting the web site URL (web address) that you would like them to visit on your business card, stationary, emails, or other communications. If anyone is trying to check you out, the Internet and social media sites are often the first places they will look.

There are many social media sites on the Internet that are geared more for business networking than personal communications. *LinkedIn* is one of the more popular sites. You can post things about yourself that are relevant to your sales career such as your education, job history, and life experiences that you would like your customers and potential customers to know about.

While honesty is the best policy, avoid posting information about past jobs and experiences that are not relevant to your current sales position. For example, if your job prior to getting hired into medical sales was working on a lawn crew, while it is nothing to be ashamed of, it is not pertinent. In fact, it may scare-off some of your customers from working with you since it screams that you're a rookie in the medical world. True, everyone needs to start somewhere, and you should not lie about your previous work experience if someone asks, but you don't need to announce it to the world unless it serves a purpose.

Be careful using social media sites where others can make comments or post pictures and videos of you without your approval. On some sites, people can "tag" a photo of you, and it shows up on your profile for the entire world to see. What you do on your time off may be your business, but if someone posts a picture of you doing something your customers might not approve of, it could harm your business and cause a company that you represent to discipline or terminate you. Photographs of you celebrating at your friend Bob's bachelor party may remind you of the great time you had, but your customers may see the depicted behavior in a different way. Things like this should be kept private and separate from your professional life, but nothing that is online is truly private. Remember, you represent each company whose products you sell, and to your customers, you *are* that company. Anything that makes you look bad makes the company look bad, and looking bad is something that few companies will tolerate. Even if you post information on sites where the only people who can see it are those people in your network, there is always a way for the information to find its way to your customers and employer. Make sure there is nothing posted on the Internet that you would not want a customer, employer, or company that you represent to see.

On occasion, I have spotted comments on social media and other Internet sites where sales reps are badmouthing their competition or responding to a negative comment about their company or products. Don't do this—it's a bad idea, for several reasons. Saying less than complimentary things about competitors does little to win approval with your customers. It makes you look weak, defensive and desperate. It can also invite a lawsuit, even if what you are saying is the truth. Always take the high road by refusing to badmouth your competitors. Sell your products by discussing the benefits with your customers one-on-one. Don't allow a competitor to suck you into an online war-of-words. Report any negative comments or postings about your company or products to the appropriate personnel at your company and let them handle the situation. Your customers will never fault you for not engaging in online mudslinging.

One of the safest ways to have an online presence where you have full control over the content is to create your own website. The website should include information that is relevant to your business and useful to your customers. If you include any product information, again, make sure it is approved by your company, or better yet, consider posting a hyperlink on your site that takes readers directly to the manufacturer's official website.

Your own website is a great way to passively build a relationship with your customers by allowing them to learn important information about you. *MySalesRep.com* is a perfect example of a medical sales professional's personal business website. They make the site very easy to set-up and charge a relatively low, monthly fee. Your site includes several pages that allow you to present yourself mainly from a professional perspective, but also personally. You can upload a good quality photograph of yourself, which helps to introduce yourself to new customers, and to remind existing customers who you are. There are places to post news and current events information, product information or a link to a corporate products website, photos of yourself that serve your professional image well (such as receiving company awards, performing community service work, etc.), references from satisfied customers, a calendar to post upcoming events in your industry and your business, and last, but certainly not least, complete contact information. Of course you could hire a webmaster, or build a site yourself, but a service such as this makes it super simple and removes the excuse of you not having the time or the money to create an online presence.

Internet Technology in Medical Sales is Here to Stay

Online technology, when used properly, can bolster your image as a medical sales professional and help you to build and maintain your base of business. It is a tool that allows you to respond to your customers' needs efficiently by delivering needed information such as product protocols, clinical studies, and ordering information almost instantly. The Internet is also a great resource for patients, who can visit company websites and learn about their conditions and treatment options in both video and printed formats.

The pharmaceutical industry has already implemented *e-detailing*, or electronically delivered drug information via the Internet to take the place of traditional in-office detailing. While more than half of the physicians surveyed indicated that they preferred e-detailing, it will be interesting to see what percentage of them actually make the time to receive online detailing for the drugs that they prescribe or are considering. While e-detailing is an efficient way to disseminate product information, it won't replace the impact that a live face-to-face presentation has, especially with products that healthcare providers want to have demonstrated in person. It is likely though, that e-detailing is here to stay.

More and more healthcare providers are asking sales people to communicate with them through email or text-messaging since it is non-intrusive and allows them to respond at a convenient time. It is also convenient to attach documents to the emails for instant review and approval by customers. Make sure you ask your customers for permission before sending emails or text-messages (sending a written message via your cell phone to their cell phone) so that you don't show up in their inboxes uninvited.

It is likely that the Internet and the associated social media sites will play a bigger role in medical sales in the years to come. This technology can help you drive sales and provide better service to your customers and their patients. Think of creative ways to use the online world to build your business, but first make sure you clear it with the appropriate personnel in your company or the companies you represent so you don't violate any regulatory or corporate compliance rules.

Final Thoughts About Mastering Medical Sales

If you have made it through this book, you know that selling in the medical arena can be very different from selling in other industries. To succeed in medical sales, you may need to do some things differently than you have in the past. It will take some effort, but I promise you, the effort will be worth it.

Healthcare and its associated industries will continue to grow well into the next decade and beyond. The selling terrain may change with time, but the need for healthcare products and services won't ever go away. The medical sales professional who performs the job well will always be employed and well-compensated.

Remember that medicine is a dynamic field and part of your job is to keep up with current trends and technologies. Sales methods may change in the future, as well. Regardless of whether or not your company provides sales and product training, increasing your knowledge and honing your selling skills is *your* responsibility. The investment for sales training and ongoing learning will pay huge dividends, and I encourage you to invest in training on your own if your company does not provide it.

Know that changes in the economy and healthcare will affect your business in the future. Even if what you have been doing has proven effective over the years, there will come a time when you will need to step back, re-evaluate and take a different approach. There may even be times when you will feel like you are starting all over again.

There is an ebb and flow to the medical sales business. Whether you are on the upswing or riding out tough times, know that it won't last. Always stay focused on your job and be committed to doing what is best for the healthcare provider and the patient, and you will not only survive; you will prosper over time.

Please remember to take advantage of all of the resources available to you. These include your sales managers, scientific journals, customers, fellow medical sales professionals, and online resources for current medical information and medical sales training, including live training seminars.

My company, Sales Pilot Medical Sales Training, and I are dedicated to helping you on your road to medical sales success. Please feel free to contact us at 561.333.8080 or visit www.MedicalSalesTraining.com.

Congratulations on your commitment to provide healthcare professionals and healthcare institutions with the products, services and associated information that they need to deliver quality patient care. You are a professional, and what you do makes a difference in people's lives.

Acknowledgments

As I reflect on the last 25 years, I see the faces of so many of the people who were all part of the experiences that made this book possible. I am grateful for those who supported me emotionally, encouraged me, challenged me, taught me, knew when to let me learn by allowing me to make my own mistakes, and when to step in and keep me from *getting hurt*. The vast majority of my experiences and interactions in medical sales have been positive and rewarding, but even those that I would like to forget served as valuable lessons about people, business, and life.

Let me first acknowledge every person who devotes a portion of their time on this planet working to improve, restore, or maintain the health of others. This includes all of the doctors, nurses, therapists, researchers, and supporting personnel who give so much of themselves. I have witnessed firsthand the triumphs and tribulations of what you do, and I admire each of you who makes patient care your top priority.

Success means nothing without someone to share it with, and often never occurs without someone who cares about you and supports your ambition. C.J. Horoff is my wife, my best friend, and my muse. Thanks for putting up with answering services, pagers, cell phones, my journeys to hospitals at all hours of the day and night, frequent traveling, and me. You've supported me in everything I have ever wanted to do from becoming a pilot to becoming a speaker. I appreciate all that you are, all that you do, and I love you.

I remember my mother as a loving person with a unique sense of humor. She often found a funny side in situations where no reasonable person would have expected one to exist. Mom taught me to find a way to laugh at those stressful moments and this has been an invaluable, sanity-saving tool throughout my life. I miss you and your silly humor.

My father, Charles Horoff, passed away when I was eight years old, and I did not get to know him well. I learned from those who knew him that he was a likeable guy and people enjoyed his personality and his wit. Whenever anyone who knew my father shares their memories of him, they always smile. Dad always treated people well, never missed an opportunity to make them laugh, and tried to have fun at whatever he was doing. The only thing he expected of people was for them to just be themselves. I wish I had a chance to know him better.

One of the best salesmen I ever met was my uncle, Arthur Rose. He loved to share stories about the interesting people he met as a salesman in the textile business for over forty years. While I did not know it at the time, he was my first "sales trainer." My personal approach to selling is based on what he taught me. Uncle Arthur was the person I would turn to whenever I needed advice or encouragement. Thank you for always being there for me. His foremost sales rule that I will always remember is, "When customers are mean, nasty, or mistreat you . . . sell them something!"

"When the student is ready, the teacher will appear" became a most fortunate reality for me when I met Steve and Dawn Siebold. They have built a mega-successful speaking business by doing all the right things for their clients and students. Spending a few days in Maui with them at the Bill Gove Speech Workshop was one of the best career decisions I ever made. I am grateful for the friendship and business advice I have received from Dawn and Steve, who have been my mentors in the speaking business, and are living examples of what I hope to achieve.

I also want to acknowledge the late Bill Gove, who has had a major impact on my speaking style, despite the fact that I never met him. Bill, your wisdom and genius lives on through the efforts of Steve and Dawn Siebold and the hundreds, if not thousands of professional speakers whose success is traceable to you. You have left behind a truly amazing legacy and continue to touch people's lives every day.

Robert Carl, III, thank you for hiring me and sharing your entrepreneurial spirit. I always thought that the world of business was boring until you opened my eyes. Thanks for taking a risk and letting me step into the world of medical sales, and for being supportive as I transitioned into the next phase of my career.

Mike Johns, you taught me more about "people skills" in business and in life, than anyone I have ever met. You managed to be one of my closest friends and my employer for many, many years, and that combination was not an easy task. Whenever I talk about "clearly defining expectations," and "under-promise and over-deliver," I will always think of you. I thank you and Debbie for allowing me to be a part of your family. Your children, Ben and Natalie are prime examples of good parenting, and it was fun watching them grow up. Thank you for sharing the good times and the success over the years.

Thank you to the hundreds of physicians, nurses, surgical technicians, central supply techs, materials managers, hospital administrators, and numerous other clinical and business personnel that I worked with over the years. You taught me what I know, and you gave me the opportunity to serve you and your patients.

Almost every medical sales rep has a customer or two who plays an important role during the early days in the business. One such customer for me was Mel Rech, D.O. Dr. Rech let me earn his business with small, commodity-type products for several years, before giving me a shot at his "big business." He mentored me through my early days of medical sales by teaching me about medicine and customer service. I will always remember his kindness and generosity.

Helen Hydock, R.N. was one of the most respected nurse-managers I have ever known, and she was a wonderful friend. Thank you for getting the doctors to open their doors to me, even though they had not seen a sales rep from my company for almost a year. Having you on my side was one of the best things that happened to me in my early career. Thank you for your friendship and for being a class act.

I worked with hundreds of excellent nurses over the years, but a few stand out because of their deep concern for each and every patient, and they were a joy for me to work with. Thank you to Carol Hanlon, R.N., Patty O'Driscoll, R.N., Carol Lombardo, R.N., Gracie Smith, R.N., Beth Suriano, R.N., Zoe Bliss, R.N., and Dale Layton Johnson, R.N. You are all special people who I will never forget.

To Lee Weston, "The Great One," thanks for teaching me "the ropes" of the business, and for leaving me many happy customers when I took over your territory.

The majority of my competitors were hard-working, honest people who set the bar for competition very high. I am grateful to them for inspiring me to work hard and for keeping me constantly challenged and on my toes.

One former competitor, Jim Hill, has become a close friend and was one of the people who encouraged me to pursue my passion of speaking and training. Now that I know Jim as a friend, I can understand why it was nearly impossible to ever convert any of his business. Thanks, Jim.

I appreciate the generosity of the medical sales professionals that I have known throughout the years, who shared with me their selling secrets and their wisdom.

To Brenda Robinson, who edited my manuscript and reassured me that my writing style is "fine," thank you for taking on this project and for being available to me throughout its completion.

Ken Harman is one of my best friends, and an amazingly talented guy. How lucky am I to have the former VP of Advertising and Creative Design for a major motion picture studio create the most visible part of my book? I'm very lucky for that, but much luckier to have had you as one of my closest, life-long friends since high school. Thanks for all of your support over the years and for designing the perfect cover.

Most people who succeed in the speaking business are part of a mastermind group. Gary Greenfield, Allison Adams Blankenship, and I meet once each month to brainstorm ideas, create action plans, and hold each other accountable. It's brutal fun! Thank you both for sharing your experience and wisdom with me, and for all the "tough love."

Several years ago, I was lucky to meet Julie Morgenstern and her business partner, Herve Jolicoeur, who offered me the opportunity to work with their organization, JME, as a facilitator for their Work*Smart, Productivity Skills for Knowledge Workers* time management workshop. The workshop has done wonders for my own personal time management challenges, and it is a joy for me to facilitate the workshop with your corporate clients. Thank you for allowing me to license the workshop and offer a version specifically geared to help people who sell in healthcare manage their time challenges. Julie, you are "The Guru" of time management and organization.

I am blessed to be surrounded by friends and neighbors who help to balance my professional life with a fun and exciting personal life. I have learned from some of the best who know how to work hard and play harder.

I could not do what I do today without the companies and organizations that invite me to speak with and train their medical, dental and pharmaceutical sales teams. Thank you for your trust in me, and for the past, present, and future opportunities to work with you.

Specialized Medical Sales Training Workshops and Keynotes

Delivered by Mace Horoff

Specifically designed for those who sell to healthcare.

Interactive, Informative, Thought-provoking, Authentic, and Results-oriented

Corporate Medical Sales Training

The people in your sales force were hired for their accomplishments, talents, and potential to drive sales for your company. Our Sales Pilot™ workshops exploit these abilities by creating an understanding of how the healthcare customer thinks when buying, and leveraging that understanding throughout the sales process. All workshops are tailored to the needs of your sales force using accelerated learning techniques to ensure that the enhanced selling skills are immediately useable upon returning to the territory. For more information, please visit **www.MedicalSalesTraining.com or call 561.333.8080**

Medical Sales Time Management

Your sales people can have the best selling skills in the world, but unless they create the time for face-to-face sales conversations, the benefits of those selling skills won't be realized. Sales Pilot™ has licensed the Work*Smart, Productivity Skills for Knowledge Workers* workshop by New York Times best-selling author and time management expert Julie Morgenstern, and tailored it for the healthcare sales and marketing professional. Workshop participants learn to take control of each day in the territory, and recover at least one hour per day to devote to critical, high-level tasks such as selling. What sales increases could your company expect if each member of your sales organization made 20 additional sales calls per month? For more information, please visit www.MedicalSalesTraining.com/time_management.htm **or call 561.333.8080**

Teleconference/Webinar Training and Coaching

Sales training must be continuously reinforced to create and maintain maximum effectiveness. We will engage your sales force on a regularly scheduled basis—weekly, bimonthly, monthly, or quarterly to ensure proficiency in their medical selling skills. During each call or webinar, your sales people will analyze the victories, losses, and existing challenges in their territories and identify opportunities as a group to create a deeper understanding of their business. Ongoing training helps to hold people accountable to do the things every day that drive sales. Programs are presented live via teleconference bridge line and as online interactive webinars. Sessions can be recorded for access by those who are unable to participate in the live call or webinar, and can also be accessed for review as often as necessary.

For information on all of our training programs and workshops, please visit **www.MedicalSalesTraining.com or call 561.333.8080**

Keynote Presentations

That celebrity, ex-football coach might be a great choice as a keynote speaker if you wanted your sales force to think like football players. Instead, why not bring in a speaker that will help them win as medical sales professionals?

Whether you have an audience of ten, or ten thousand, Mace Horoff captures the listeners' attention and takes them on a journey in their own world—the world of medical sales. Mace's keynotes are informative, entertaining, and tailored to each client's specifications.

To learn more about Mace Horoff's keynote presentations, please visit **www.MedicalSalesSpeaker.com or call 561.333.8080**

Public Medical Sales Training Seminars

Sales Pilot™ offers medical sales training seminars for individual attendees at various times and locations throughout the year. These are ideal for new medical sales representatives, current medical sales representatives who wish to strengthen their medical selling skills, companies that desire training for only a few representatives, or job candidates who are looking to increase their chances of getting hired in medical sales.

For information on public medical sales training programs, please visit www.MedicalSalesTraining.com or call Sales Pilot at 561.333.8080.

FREE Ezine, Medical Sales Podcasts and Videos

To receive *The Medical Sales Achiever* ezine, medical sales podcasts and videos that are full of valuable information for medical sales professionals, including the video *How to Get Past the Gatekeeper and Get in to See the Doctor*, please subscribe for free at **www.Medical SalesTraining.com/gatekeeper.htm**

Index